HOW TO ANALYZE
& REVIEW COMICS

A HANDBOOK ON COMICS CRITICISM

HOW TO ANALYZE & REVIEW COMICS

A HANDBOOK ON COMICS CRITICISM

EDITED BY

FORREST C. HELVIE

SEQUART ORGANIZATION   EDWARDSVILLE, ILLINOIS

How to Analyze & Review Comics: A Handbook on Comics Critcism
edited by Forrest C. Helvie

Cover by Julian Darius and Jim Wilcox. Book design by Julian Darius. Interior art is © its respective owners.

Published by Sequart Organization. Edited by Forrest C. Helvie.

For more information about other titles in this series, visit Sequart.org/books.

Contents

Acknowledgements

First, I want to acknowledge and thank the contributors to *How to Analyze and Review Comics*, without whom this project would never have come together. You have offered infinite patience as we navigated many life challenges that delayed its release, and I look forward to the discussions your work will engender amongst the comics community and beyond.

Second, I want to thank the generous comics storytellers who offered their time to be interviewed for this volume: Becky Cloonan, Michael Avon Oeming, FCO Plascencia, Rachel Deering, Brian Michael Bendis, Comfort Love, Adam Withers, Jim Zub, Jose Villarubia, Hannah Means-Shannon, and Andy Schmidt. No critic worth their salt operates in a vacuum, and your insights into comics will no doubt help many critics, commentators, students, and journalists better understand and discuss the medium that we love so much.

Next, I want to send a special thank you to the students in my past ENG 274: Comics as Literature courses at Norwalk Community College, who had the opportunity to use early drafts of this text in their course. Your feedback and responses were incredibly helpful in bringing this book together in its final form.

Additionally, I would be remiss to not thank the comics press editors I have had the privilege to work with over the years. At Newsarama, David Pepose and Chris Arrant's constant guidance and feedback helped me produce some of my best interviews and written comic critiques. Pep also gave me big break as a "big time" reviewer and critic, and I'll always be grateful. At Marvel, Ben Morse brought my writing back to basics and helped me developed even further. Without a doubt, I am a better writer and critic for their support and input.

Finally, I want to offer a special thanks to my publisher, Julian Darius, and Sequart's Editor in Chief, Mike Phillips. You both gave me my first opportunity to write about comics years ago on Sequart.org, and it feels fitting that my first scholarly text about comics criticism should find its home at Sequart. I cannot thank you enough for all of the hours of support you both provided in bringing this collection to life.

And as always, much love to my wife and sons. Any writer knows that time spent writing often comes at the cost of time spent away from one's family. I could have never done this without your support and love.

Forrest C. Helvie
Editor

Introduction: Thoughts on Reviewing Comics

by Forrest C. Helvie

> Don't forget the rules, man. This little shit is the enemy. He writes what he sees…. although it would be cool to be on the cover.
> — *Almost Famous* (2000).

Is this a one-star or a five-star comic? What really is a perfect "10"?

Every Wednesday, local comic shops and online retailers provide readers with a bevy of new comic book titles and issues. Some superhero series take flight while others crash without rhyme or reason. Some of us who bear witnesses to these initial successes and failures are likely to write the occasional reviews on these comics. Other readers, however, growing tired of the "superhero boom" and move onto other genres to read and write about.

Perhaps you're not a "Wednesday Warrior" and have been assigned a graphic novel to read – either as a part of a class or your news editor assigned it to you. Maybe comics are a somewhat or altogether unfamiliar format for reading and beyond writing about the story, you're not sure how exactly to go about discussing the art.

So how do we go about performing this task of writing about comics, especially when there are many different genres of this four-colored medium and our experience with reading comics from an analytical perspective may be limited? Is there a science to determining whether a given comic's first issue has the right "stuff" to be the next big thing – or at the very least, continue selling for another few months? How do we know whether or not an ongoing series has slowly begun nose-diving or, instead, is moving into a brave, new world of creative storytelling? How do we approach a graphic novel that does not appeal to mainstream sensibilities in its art and narrative direction?

Not surprisingly, there is no one surefire answer to how to review a comic. I've written for mainstream sites, such as Marvel.com and Newsarama, to more academic journals and publications, and without fail, many of the writers from these different publishers approach their funny books from a variety of different perspectives. However, there are certain characteristics many of us try to keep in mind when applying a critical lens to comics of all shapes and sizes.

While we all have our opinions, they're not necessarily going to have the same value. After all, it's one thing to steer readers away from poorly a conceived and created comic – it's another thing altogether when a critic unfairly skews other readers' opinions against a new book when it probably deserves a more even-handed review. What you will find in this collection are just a few points from across the spectrum of comics – from academics and journalists to professional creators – that you should consider before drafting a paper for one of your English classes, writing up that next scathing review for a personal blog, posting some comments to a message board, or even just in passing conversation with fellow fans at the local comic shop. Although this handbook makes no assertion that it will cover every element, we hope it will provide a solid place to launch a more thoughtful and informed discussion about comics and their ability to convey narrative in ways altogether different from other forms of storytelling.

Comics is a visual medium, so there's no escaping the fact the art needs to be good. But that's a loaded word, isn't it? Good. How does one measure taste in a broad sense when aesthetic interest is so highly subjective? Simple – we do our best to avoid overly broad terms like that. So how do comic readers learn to speak about the artwork?

Before digging into the collected essays in this text, I'd like to share some other resources I've used to increase my understanding behind the process that goes into making comics and the different ways the medium functions. These sources have helped – I'd like to think – to improve the level of critical analysis that I bring to my comic reviews and analysis. It's certainly not comprehensive, but it does provide some key sources of reading and experience worth pursuing:

- Scott McCloud's *Understanding Comics*. Required reading that provides a formalist breakdown of comics and comics theory. I also have two of his other books – *Reinventing Comics* and *Making Comics* – and while the mileage varies on these two (*Reinventing Comics* sometimes showing its age), I've still found them useful and informative all the same.

- Jessica Abdel and Matt Madden's *Drawing Words and Pictures* and *Mastering Comics*. These two books are essentially two independent self-studies on making comics and incredibly accessible.

- Will Eisner's *Instructional Book Series*. This is one of the industry's greatest legends, and these books formed the basis for the classes he taught in NY on comics studies. If you can only get one, go with *Graphic Storytelling and Visual Narrative* as it is perhaps most relevant to academics and journalists alike.

- The Internet. I also know there are a LOT of good articles posted online about how to review comics. David Harper (Mulitversity, Sktchd) along with Hass Otsmane-Elhaou's *PanelXPanel* publication and Strip Panel Naked Youtube Channel provide two examples of some excellent comics criticism.

- Comic Conventions. Go talk to artists. Ask them what sort of feedback has been the most beneficial and informative to them. As a comics critic, I'm not trained in the fine arts, so I am not able to provide that level of feedback in my reviews. That said, I've learned a lot about what to look for artistically by chatting about the form with artists at various conventions.

- Make Your Own Comics. In all honesty, you'll learn a lot and gain a fuller appreciation for what these artists and writers are doing by attempting to create your own comic story. It doesn't have to be long either – just seeing what it's like being the writer, being the penciller the inker, the colorist, the letterer. And when you're done, go look at one of the comics you purchased off the newsstand and reverse-engineer that issue. Not only will you have a greater appreciation for the process, but you'll have a little more understanding of how the parts of the comic work (and don't work when done poorly from having done so firsthand).

There are also a number of more recent books out there from well-known creators and editors such as Brian Michael Bendis' *Words for Pictures*, Andy Schmidt's *The Insider's Guide to Creating Comics and Graphic Novels*, Comfort Love and Adam Withers' *The Complete Guide to Self-Publishing Comics* and many others. Each of these books covers much of the same ground, but does so from a variety of perspectives from within the industry that will better enable its readers to understand the many aspects of what makes a comic book tick. Pick one, check it out, and apply what you've learned. Next, try and describe what the artist did on the page (or attempted to accomplish) before assessing his or her success. I tell my first-year writing students that knowledge application can be stressful, as they'll make mistakes at first; however, they'll discover they're improving in their craft as they commit to practicing it on a regular basis.

What's more is many creators do read online reviews and articles, and I'd like to think (foolishly / naively) some of them are listening carefully to what we have to say. For many students reading this, understand that the term paper you write today could be your next published article for an indie news outlet. For writers at smaller news outlets, you never know when a creator or publisher you reviewed will see what you wrote. And for those writing for the larger sites, thousands – if not millions – of readers will see your work, so you want to look and sound as professional as possible. So before you hit "Post" or "Send" and air your review for the world, try to make sure you're not leaving out the people who are responsible for the defining characteristic of this medium: The artists and their art. Be brave and take a risk by talking about those parts of the comic that are intimidating. Keep doing it until you get better. What all of this boils down to, however, is when analyzing a comic from a critical perspective, it's important to be able to use precise vocabulary to address specific elements of the comic in question. Otherwise, it's just vague, subjective, and doesn't give any indication where the specific strengths and weaknesses lie.

Shifting gears a bit, I want to take a look back at when I first read *The Watchmen*, which provides a good example of how learning about the craft of creating comics can actually increase one's ability to enjoy the medium. I confess that I did not enjoy the aesthetic of Dave Gibbons when I first read this landmark comic. I preferred more stylized superhero renditions as seen in John Romita Jr., Mike Zeck, Alan Davis, and other contemporaries of that day. Since that time, however, I have since grown to appreciate his mastery of panel composition and line control that help deliver the clean and controlled "flavor" that permeates this milestone mini-series. An example of this can be seen best, arguably, in the scene on Mars when Dr. Manhattan creates a clock-like construct only to let Laurie experience its destruction. Gibbons (through Dr. Manhattan) presents a construct of inhuman design and a feat of engineering unmatched by anything mankind had ever been able to create. And tragically, it could not last in the world of *The Watchmen* – something the visual elements clearly communicate.

Now, after learning how comics work and observing how well-executed Gibbons' work is, I have a difficult time not enjoying each panel he composed for this series. After all, one of the grand and cruel jokes of *Watchmen* centers on is how the chaos these heroes encounter throughout the story is really a secretly orchestrated plan that will not only have consequences directly in opposition to their desired goals as heroes, but one in which they will implicitly participate: Chaos all under the grand control of another – both the plan of Ozymandias, but also the book's creative team.

So, what does my interest in Dave Gibbons' work have to do with analyzing comics beyond increasing my enjoyment of them as a reader? In the example above, I mentioned one of the major themes of the book and provide at least one example related to the artist's line work to support the argument. It's not a lot of support, but in a review, it's important to avoid giving all of the details away and spoiling the experience for new readers. Nonetheless, a claim never goes without specific support. Let's look at another example.

Opposite to someone like Dave Gibbons, from an aesthetic standpoint, would be an artist such as Sam Keith. His wild and animalistic depictions of superheroes such as Wolverine, The Incredible Hulk, and The Maxx tapped into the uncontrollable, bestial elements of these dangerous beings. He made use of sprawling, tattered clothes that barely covered their robust, hairy bodies. His superhero renditions served as a visual reminder to my young eyes that not all heroes were "safe." His artwork is well-known for its heavy inks with torn and tattered costumed heroes often set against a wilderness that threatened to engulf them. Readers were brought down a hole not so dissimilar from the one Alice took when she entered into the acid trip-inspired Wonderland. Unlike Gibbons, Keith's style eschews the clean and controlled line of the real world for a rough edge and hyper-real representation of the persons inhabiting his world with pages that often broke with tradition. He filled panels with characters dropping from heights on the top of the page plummeting to the bottom panel in a sort of splash with some panels strewn about as though an after-effect of the explosive energy. The artistic elements in his comics lend themselves to a world that was bigger, darker, other-worldly, and more dangerous than the one in which I sat safely reading my comic book.

Certainly, one cannot escape the ways an artist's inks and use of panel and page composition affect the tone and mood of the comics as I've tried to touch upon here. Notice that I attempt to use specific and concreate word choices, which help my reader visualize what I'm describing with choices that point towards the quality of the work such as "animalistic" "heavy inks," and "rough-edge" all of which help point to the style Keith employs. More academic pieces will no doubt need to provide further discussion while more mainstream sources, often working within more confined article lengths, will simply need to select the most powerful examples for analysis. But either way, dig in and be specific about the art!

A third and final example of how one might review the artistic form of a comic can be seen in Charles Burns with his use of a woodcut style to his artwork as exemplified in *Black Hole*, which was originally published at first in the traditional, single-issue form. He works strictly with solid black ink and white fill in this offbeat coming of age story dealing with sex and mutation. It's a smart choice because – as most people discover – when sex enters the discussion, it's rarely a black and white issue. In this regard, there is a sort of irony over the use of such stark contrast in color when there are a host of issues discussed where people would find themselves occupying more "gray" areas than either black or white in relation to the challenges facing the characters in the story. So while Burns art might lack the visual excitement of a Sam Keith, or cinematic-like composition of Gibbons, his own approach through presenting this somewhat realistic story – not without a significant number of surreal twists and turns – provides yet another instance of how the artistic elements can still be employed with deliberate intention in smart, thought-provoking ways. Form and artistic style come together to convey certain ideas to or evoke specific emotional responses from their readers regardless of whether the reader "likes" how it looks. It's a classic example of where form fits the purpose.

Those are just a few examples of the different elements comics critics and reviewers often pay attention to when reading a comic for more than entertainment purposes – though being able to better appreciate the artistic craft can and will no doubt enhance many readers' appreciation and enjoyment of a well-crafted story. And speaking of story... let's face it: it might look nice, but if it's not saying much, readers' are going to treat that comic like a bad date and walk away after the first outing.

All stories have to be about something. Characters need to be involved and they need to be involved in some sort of conflict – whether internal, external, or both. If there are no problems or challenges to face, then readers have little opportunity for excitement in their story. Likewise, many readers look to literature – prose or comic – to engage in a sort of cultural discourse, that is, they often want to see solutions to the problems and cares they face in the real world played out in their works of fiction. There is a desire to encounter characters whom they can relate to or learn from. Absent any conflict, the story fails to provide the reader with this opportunity in a substantive way. So, stories need some form of conflict to drive the character(s) into motion.

That said, there are many different types of conflict that writers and reviewers should be aware of, but of course, critics continually differ on the kinds of literary conflict to be found: Are there four kinds? Are there seven? By and large, some of the most commonly accepted forms include: Man v. Self, Man v. Man, Man v. Society, Man v. Nature, Man v. the Supernatural, and Man v. Technology. Further, narratives will often contain multiple story threads with different types of conflict playing out as the narrative develops. It's the critic's job to tease out these threads and determine how effective and compelling they were woven together.

Moreover, if readers are to spend any period of time with these characters, the people they read about will need a certain amount of character development to provide a more three-dimensional representation of these people. This means we learn backstory: What brought the main character to the place where we, the readers, are now meeting them? What motivates him or her to risk (or avoid!) conflict? The writer creates points in the character's development that allow us to relate to this fictional being and therefore invest in his or her well-being. Flat characters are stereotypes, and most readers are all-too-familiar with who these characters are, what motivates them, and recognize what growth – if any – will occur with them by the end of the story. As a result, there's little reason to be all that interested in these sorts of protagonists and even antagonists. We may not get all of this information right away, of course; however, these are questions that will eventually need to be addressed in one form or another.

The last element that is really important for a good story is consistency. It's the stuff that helps bind both characters and conflicts in a narrative. No, I'm not talking about the "foolish" sort that Ralph Waldo Emerson railed against. In fact, most people erroneously believe that Emerson was a stalwart against consistency when he said "A foolish consistency is the hobgoblin of little minds," which is actually quite incorrect. It was a mindset of unthinking persistence in the same course of behaviors he thought wrong-minded. But in terms of storylines and consistency? Not so. Smartly constructed world building – the very stuff of the very best stories – demonstrates consistency.

In his work "On Fairy Stories," J.R.R. Tolkien discussed the absolute necessity that a writer not only establishes a set of rules for the world he or she was crafting, but that these rules are consistently followed within the realm of that story. To break these rules, a writer would effectively jar readers out of the world of imagination from which they were immersed, make them aware of the fiction they were reading, and fall short of delivering a surrealistic reading experience.

That's the problem with seeing a *deus ex machina* – "God in the Machine," which occurs when a writer suddenly changes the rules of that world without previously having hinted at the outcome's possibility to ensure a certain event takes place. When character suddenly demonstrates magical powers or is whisked away from danger without any sensible explanation, the dissonance the audience experiences is that of a deus ex machina. Likewise, story threads that are started but left unresolved also violate the reader's need for consistency, and can result in an unsatisfying and lesser reading experience. "Checkov's Gun" refers to the notion that if we see a loaded weapon on the mantle, it must be fired before then end of the story; otherwise, it's a waste of time and a tease to the reader to have introduced it. Thus, a writer who can inject fresh perspectives on old characters or stories while still maintaining a consistent spirit is one who can be viewed as having achieved at least some measure of success in his or her storytelling.

Characters, conflict, and consistency. There is a lot more to a good story, I know, but for my part, these are perhaps the three most important ingredients to a compelling narrative. The "where" and "when" can change from the antiquities of the past to the distant reaches of a galaxy, far, far away. When we talk about developing character, hearing from them through smartly chosen dialogue or interior monologues through captions can go a long way to helping drive the story, or even better, showing who they are through their actions and interactions with others. And the purposes a writer might choose to embed within the story are too many to count. But a story cannot be told without characters and conflict. The other need only ensure they are discussed in a consistent way that adds to the reader's experience, and does not shake them out of the fictional world they seek to enter. As a reviewer, these are some of the main elements I look for when analyzing a comic and determining its weaknesses and strengths.

Ultimately, critics and reviewers should attempt to provide an analysis of the different elements of the comic being reviewed from the narrative to the visual aspects. At the end of the day, however, it is still an opinion even if it does appear to be a valid one. The difference between a well-written review and the stereotypical internet troll is where one writer tries to take pains to show what elements of the writer and artist's work were especially enjoyable (or unsatisfactory) and why the elicited the type of response that they did. The other simply complains without any valid support, and few ever take them seriously. For my part, I generally adhere to the rule that if you can't say anything nice about a comic, then don't review it. While I realize there is value to making readers aware of "lemons" on the newsstand, I'm equally aware that making comics is an excruciatingly difficult business. Regardless of whether I connect with a particular comic, it's important to recognize the efforts that went into its creation. And sometimes, silence serves as the best form of negative criticism.

The approach outlined above is one I use to try and focus on critiquing the work, and not the creator. Even if people disagree with my analysis, which is going to happen, at least it treats the comic with respect. And that's something that matters a good deal. After all, you never know if the words you write will get back to the person who helped write or draw that comic.

Of course, this is a just the tip of the iceberg when it comes to what goes into attempting a critical review of a comic. There are many writers far more skilled and articulate in their analyses, and I regularly look to them for pointers on how I might better communicate my thoughts and treatment of the comic books I continue to read day in and out. It's easy to simply assign a numerical rating to a comic, but sitting down and writing as fair and as balanced a review as possible is a far more valuable thing. I hope this helps.

As we wrap things up, it bears repeating that in no way do I claim that what this handbook provides is anything close to comprehensive. Instead, I'm only looking to "start a conversation" with this framework and provide some basic examples of talking about comic art. Because this collection of essays and interviews is aimed primarily for those interested in writing about comics, I wanted to have a few individuals share some thoughts on the work they do. Some of these discussions will be quick-draw interviews where I ask comics professionals three questions about their respective craft. Other interviews are deeper dives into that professional's field and how the significance of comics criticism from their perspective. Still others are full articles written by comics professionals, journalists, academics, and creators that will touch upon the many different aspects of comics along with providing a handful of useful approaches in analyzing comics today.

So let's dive in, shall we?

In Defense of Comics Criticism: Why We Need Analysis

by Hassan Otsmane-Elhaou

When you watch Penn & Teller do their particular brand of magic, it taps into something innate in us as a viewer. We want to pull the curtain back, we want to see the reality, how the magic happens. So probably the first response you'll hear after a trick is, "How did you do that?!"

The beauty of a Penn & Teller trick is often we do get to see how they did it, and that the reveal is just as imaginative and interesting as the magic itself.

It's still entertainment.

Just like magic, understanding how comics work is pretty useful for anyone that wants to discuss them, write them, draw them, or be involved with them in some capacity. And like magic, the resources for learning this have often been difficult to get into. As a reader of comics, I struggled with accessible writing about the medium that hit the spot, because a lot of analysis falls back onto the same few works again and again, or more niche, less mainstream work. Or, more likely, the writing around it is incredibly academic. Mostly my initial learning came from the same place most people's did, from just trying to make comics as a kid.

The problem with that is, like magic, there is a lot to learn about the craft of comics, what approaches and methods you can use and adapt in your work, that will get missed or not engaged with. So you immediately end up playing catch up, or worse, never even engaging with whole aspects of the medium. Plenty of comics readers who have been fans for decades don't see the artistry and creative decision making that goes into lettering, for example, something they interact with constantly in every comic they've read. We need to find ways to see this is important.

I have a background in filmmaking, and I studied it at university. Though it was almost exclusively a practical course, the first thing they taught us was how to view films from a theoretical and critical viewpoint. How to look at the decisions a film was making, through color choice, shots, lens selection, duration, mise en scène and more. It was a big breakthrough moment in realising that it's not just the A-to-B narrative that holds weight in films, because just as (if not more in some cases) important is the way it's being presented. Even though I thought I had a handle on this already, it was a revelation.

I see analysis as a tool to kind of reverse-engineer work and see how something performs the function it's aiming for (or falls short of that goal). It's more useful as a creator – though as a reader I get a kick out of seeing how a bunch of ink on paper made me genuinely emote – aiming to deliver something that sparks an idea or kickstarts the imagination and gets the motor whirring. It's about increasing the tricks and techniques in your toolbox, adding to your own functionality as a storyteller in the medium. It's just that often the approach to getting started doing this is a mystery.

In fact, the question I've probably been asked most since starting *Strip Panel Naked* and *PanelxPanel* is: How do I learn to be analytical? And I think a big part of that is because mostly this work has been behind closed doors as academic texts.

Doing that shuts off interesting work and ideas, and it closes off accessibility into understanding the medium, which to me is key in developing an approach to it as both a critic and a creator. I'm a firm believer that being able to deconstruct and decode other works is really, really useful in taking your own work to the next level. And as a critic or reviewer, how are you going to discuss the purpose of the work without being able to see how it's doing what it's doing? Film and television have been leading accessible analysis on their mediums for a long, long time, and the advent of YouTube and the open resources on the internet, as well as a huge growth in media education at every level has opened up our understanding of how it works. Nowadays, we're all pretty media savvy.

Comics still have a lot of catching up to do in that regard, and that's a big factor in why I started the *Strip Panel Naked* series on YouTube (and later *PanelxPanel* magazine). I wanted to take modern, mainstream works in comics – which means a lot of superhero books – and take a look at how they worked, hopefully creating a place for others to learn along with me. The aim was always to do it in a way that was interesting, entertaining and straight-forward. I found that removing yourself as a critic from work like this was useful, in that it's about the work you're discussing more than it is about the person talking about it, and trying to focus the work at the forefront of all of it.

By collecting an ever-growing series of resources, it was a way for me to learn more about how comics work with real-world examples from work that was still happening right now, and mixing that with work that was seen as historically interesting. It was also a way to put that out into the world to get other people who want to make comics thinking in a similar way, thinking about how they can use some of these tools in their own work, apply it to their own thinking or criticism, too. I've had a lot of feedback from working professionals and educators that they use the channel as a valuable resource, as well as from the community around it of aspiring creators. This is the benefit of accessible analysis in generating discussion.

I think it all comes down to appreciation of the medium. People love comics for different reasons, but if you want to write about comics, I truly believe it's important to see how they work. If your goal is to be able to be critical about their function and approach (which I believe the role of creator also falls into), understanding the various parts of the medium, the options creators have and decisions they make, is vital.

It makes the experience of the work even more interesting. To bring in the magic analogy once again, when I see a trick performed well I'm in awe. When I find out how it's done, it doesn't ruin the magic for me. Instead it makes the performance, the approach, the trickery, even more interesting, because I can see the work that has gone into it. Suddenly it's changed from something I don't understand to something made up of various parts and mechanisms, the patter of the magician interacting with the sleight of hand to create something special – that's what captures my excitement. With comics it's the same. The finished article is one thing, and it stands on its own, but being able to see the working parts, the way that sequence adapts it's visuals across a three-panel tier, or how a splash page uses the physicality of a printed page to speak louder than the preceding panels, that's what makes me want to spend even more time with the work.

Chances are if you're reading this, that might apply to you, too.

And when we present these to the audience, which is a mix of those creators, those aspiring creators, and the general reading audience, we're saying it's okay to look at comics this way. You can be thoughtful about your approach, and the decisions being made on the page, because you see it all here very clearly. We're saying that comics aren't these mystical things that just appear on the page, the ink lines and color just suddenly bursting into creation, but in fact are very constructed pieces of work with clear intention and design. And you're doing it because it improves the medium for the next creator. You're putting a defined impact on the way that creator might approach their next work, and so, through this, you're helping to change comics.

I'm a firm believer this all happens because the work is accessible. If it's not, who is it even for?

Getting Down to Basics: Line Art, Inking, Colors, and Lettering

Comics are more than just what happened in a story. They are *how* the story happens. Critics of all backgrounds – students, academics, and journalists alike – all need to be able to talk about the parts of a comic and the most basic elements that go into a story told in comics form include line art, inks, colors, and lettering.

99 Ways to Tell a Story

by Scott Cederlund

Every medium of storytelling has its own choices that are unique to it. In television, traditional shows shows are structured around commercial breaks. Cinema has a large canvas of a movie screen to frame its composition. With no general time or space restrictions like movies or televisions, the plot and pacing of a novel is a completely different beast with its own challenges and opportunities. Even within the broad terms of those mediums, there are a nearly infinite number of types of cinema, television, and novels that each have their own different types of decisions that have to be made. Like those mediums, comics have elements that are peculiar just to comics such as panels, word balloons, and the empty gutter space that exists between panels. In his 2005 book *99 Ways to Tell a Story: Exercises in Style*, Matt Madden explores just what those choices mean in telling a comic story.

99 times over the course of 99 pages, Madden tells the same story over and over, no two tellings are exactly the same. In his introduction to the book, Madden already begins exploring the choices that were made with his very first version titled "Template." "Yet, even a moment's consideration yields a series of questions: Why is it drawn in pen and not with a brush? Why is it told in eight panels and how were they chosen? The style is not 'cartoony,' yet is is not quite 'realistic – Why?" These are just a few of the questions that could be explored with a very straightforward story of a man finishing up work and being asked by someone upstairs "what time is it? Madden continues in the introduction, "Suddenly it's clear that what appear to be merely 'stylistic' choices are in fact an essential part of the story. In reading these comics you have the opportunity to question the effects that ways of telling have on what is being told, and, just as important, to enjoy the rich variety of approaches available to the artist, in comics and in other media."

When we read a comic book, whether we are conscious of it or not, what we're reading is the result of an almost infinite number of choices being made by everyone involved in the creation of the comic. From the editor who first has to decide whether to greenlight a new revival of Nova or to add another title to the Superman line of comics, all the way through to the colorist who has to choose just the right way to illuminate a scene, every comic book is composed through an untold number of gut instincts, second guesses, and even some mistakes that have been made along the way. It is these choices that define a creator's style. After a while, these choices repeat and become a method. The method leads to a creator's style and to a reader's recognition of that style. We begin to discover creators whose choices we like and end up following them from project to project. We also find creators whose styles just never click with us. Whether you follow creators or characters, engaging with comics is about engaging with the decisions that writers, artists, colorists, letterers, and editors have made during the creation of their story.

Often as readers, we approach comics as a writer's medium. Maybe this is some holdover from our days in high-school English classes where we picked apart stories in book reports and explored themes as if they were the purview only of serious novelists and poets. From there, it is easy to carry over a simplistic auteur point of view into most kinds of art which involve narrative and usually, that auteur is credited as one person. In movies, it's often the director who gets the credit or blame for a movies' essence. Television is called "a writer's medium." Comics can often be just by one person and some people believe that to be the purest expression of the medium. Charles Schulz wrote and drew decades worth of classic daily *Peanuts* strips by himself or Frank Miller's *Sin City* is the undiluted point of view of Miller with only a bit of help from colorist Lynn Varley. On the flipside, the synthesis of a writer and an artist's combined efforts produced a range of seminal comics from Stan Lee & Jack Kirby's *Fantastic Four* run to Grant Morrison and Frank Quitely's *Flex Mentallo*.

In his book, Madden questions the choices made from both a writer's and an artist's perspective. The first telling of the story has a simple, straightforward approach to it. In fact, it is fairly generic as there are no real daring choices made in it. The top tier of three panels shows a man getting up from his work desk. In the second tier, again, three panels but of slightly varying widths from the top tier, he's asked by an off-panel voice, "What time is it?" "It's 1:15," he replies. The final tier, only two panels this time, shows him opening his refrigerator and wondering what it was that he was looking for, anyway? There's nothing really all that mystifying or groundbreaking happening in those eight panels.

As Madden states in his introduction, even in its narrative simplicity, there are a lot of questions worth asking about those eight panels. In addition to the ones he asked, you could ask why was only a second voice heard but the asker never seen? Why did the cartoonist shift the panel orientation a bit in every tier of the page? For each consecutive panel, why did the cartoonist slightly shift the angle at which we're viewing this man? When most of the panels are close-up or medium shots of the man, why is there one panel that's a closeup of the man's hand opening the refrigerator door?

There is nothing special about this first strip of the book but in those eight panels, there are at least eight different decisions that were made in the layout and composition of this story. There were eight more decisions made about what should happen in each of those panels. The writer and artists make all of these decisions on each and every page they draw and, consciously or subconsciously, the reader engages with these decisions and choices as they read the page. In comics, the reader participates far differently in the action and motion of the story than they do in other mediums. The gutter in between the panels practically demands the reader to fill in the time from one moment or panel to the next. And for all of those small decisions made in just in those first eight panels, Madden revisits each one and finds much more with each different variation of the story.

Madden's book explores that constant push and pull between the creator and the audience, one page at a time. In each of the subsequent 98 retellings of that same story, Madden is making distinct choices about the hows of the comic while challenging the reader to ask questions about the whys of the creator's' choices. The second telling of the story, instead of depicting the events of the plot, show the man at some point after everything happened, seated at a table, drinking a cup of coffee and recounting what happened. The third telling is all from his perspective and the fourth is from the person upstairs who asks what time it is. After that, things get stranger with the fifth, where the reader is put inside of the refrigerator, kept in the dark and hearing only muffled voices until the refrigerator door is opened.

As each retelling is a new challenge for Madden, they are also new challenges for the readers. Each retelling provokes a different engagement with the reader that reflects our own engagement with the different comics we read. In Madden's variations on the theme, he tells them in ways that look like all different types of comics and we can see the effect of these styles and choices on our own reading experiences. Sometimes those experiences are reflective and sometimes they are boisterous. They may be cartoony or they may be realistically detailed. But each version of Madden's story is a distinct unit in itself that even though they share the same plot, the narrative is different because of the choices.

Now we don't see this kind of repeated variation on a theme often within the pages of a single comic. Instead of 99 different retellings of the same story, we find on comic shop racks 99 different stories told in 99 different ways. We find comedies and dramas. We find books that are slices of life and books that are the wildest of fantasies. There are comics that are very detailed and comics whose artwork are loose and improvisational. Even within comics by consistent creative teams, we can find stylistic choices that bend of shift the narrative. Madden's examples show us just a slice of the possibilities in comics. His examples with their short and descriptive titles, leave it to his readers to explore their own reactions to his story and his narrative modifications to it.

Madden's *99 Ways to Tell a Story* is the theories of Scott McCloud's *Understanding Comics* explored in a very practical way. In McCloud's 1993 book, his explorations of the ways that comics function provide a language to talk about the choices and methods of comic creators. McCloud's book has always been a fascinating study of comics because it is a comic itself and there are a lot of ways his thoughts on comics are so nonchalantly illustrated through the visual avatar of McCloud. This is not like one of Will Eisner's books where Eisner professorially approached the exploration of his theories through text and illustration. It's often overlooked that McCloud's trilogy of books – *Understanding Comics*, *Reinventing Comics*, and *Making Comics* – are comics themselves. He is telling the story of comics using the methods that he himself was exploring in the works.

Madden's book is the spiritual successor to McCloud's trilogy of books, putting many of McCloud's theories into practices. In doing so, Madden continues to define the language of comics for creators and for readers. As he changes styles and even genres of the comic, Madden shows the possibilities that exist for storytelling in general and for comics in particular but he's letting his readers discover those possibilities for themselves. His ideas about a nearly infinite canvas for storytelling are largely left unsaid. He's practicing the old adage of showing and not telling, which itself is a lesson in storytelling. It was a storytelling choice for Madden to explore this book using comics, offering little commentary about each comic other than its title. Even those choices open up the reading experience of these comics, giving the reader the room to explore their own reactions and experiences with Madden's work.

Most comics make their decisions up front and carry them through for the length of an issue, of a graphic novel, or even over the length of a career. In his book, Madden has to make a new decision every page. Even after 50 or 60 times telling the story, some of the choices are less radical than others. In one called "The Next Day," Madden recalls the events of his story, following his dialogue and even the composition of his template fairly closely. But a few pages before that is a version of it called "No Pictures (after Kenneth Koch)" that it could be debated whether it's even a comic or not. By exploring almost 100 ways that a story could be told, Madden exposes both creative processes and audience interactions that are possible. These possibilities are always present in every story but Madden illuminates their effects both on creativity and reception.

The Role of Line Art in Advancing Stories in Comics

by Sarah Cooke

Comic books are an excellent medium to study in a classroom setting for a number of reasons. One of which is the ways that the visual elements interact with and help to propel the story. There is sometimes the assumption that the artwork, and specifically the line art, is merely an illustration of the action or the dialog. Many of us are familiar with the classic (and in many ways problematic) *Dick and Jane* books, in which the artwork merely provides a visual representation of the narration. The narrative, for example, might read, "See Dick run," and the artwork on the page is a picture of Dick running. Some assume that the artwork in comics functions in a similar – albeit less rudimentary – manner. But this is not the case.

In fact, the artwork is as much of a storytelling device as the dialog and narration. The artwork serves both to tell the story, and to develop the characters. There are many techniques that artists use to achieve this, and this article will discuss a few of the primary ones.

One factor is the style of the artwork. Take a look at some of the early superhero comics. Think *Batman* or *Captain America* from, say, the Golden Age of comics (roughly the 1930s through 1960s). What you'll notice is that the panels are, for the most part, all the same size, and arranged in tidy rows. This means that each panel is given the same weight and importance in terms of its role in the story. You'll also notice that the artwork is fairly flat. That is, there's not a lot of dimension given to it. It looks less three-dimensional than more contemporary comic book art. Some of this had to do with the limitations of the production process at the time, as well as the fact that the medium had not yet fully matured. But, this style of flat, rather non-realistic artwork was actually perfectly suited for the kinds of comics that were popular at the time. Those old comics were a little campy, a little heavy handed, but that wasn't a mistake. And the artwork, which was itself perhaps lacking in some of the nuance we see today, helped create comics with that kind of tone. Many comic book readers still enjoy those comics because they form the foundation of what we see in superhero comics today. The aesthetics of the superhero comic that so many readers enjoy, and that contemporary superhero comics riff off of, have roots in those old comics, which were what they were largely due to the style of artwork.

We can see the impact of artistic style in more contemporary comics, as well. For example, take a look at *Lumberjanes*, by Shannon Watters, Grace Ellis, Brooke A. Allen, and Noelle Stevenson. It also has a relatively flat style, but not in the way that the old Golden Age comics were flat. The characters are drawn in an almost cartoonish manner, with exaggerated face and body shapes. The style is intentionally not mimetic, because this is what is called for in terms of the kind for story being told. *Lumberjanes* is about a group of girls at summer camp, whose experiences help them to discover who they really are. Although there are some tense moments and some serious subjects being dealt with, the story by and large is a somewhat quirky one about children coming into their own. A highly realistic artistic style here would not be appropriate.

Art by Brooke A. Allen from *Lumberjanes* #1 (2014).

By contrast, look at the 2016-2017 run of *Black Widow* comics, by Mark Waid and Chris Samnee. The artistic style here is much more realistic. The characters are drawn with comparatively natural body proportions and facial features, and the art has more of a sense of three-dimensionality. This makes sense, because it is a book about spies and espionage. To employ the more cartoonish style of *Lumberjanes* here would not be effective.

Art by Chris Samnee from *Black Widow* #9 (2016).

Of course, there are many factors that go into developing the overall style of the artwork. For example, *Moon Girl and Devil Dinosaur*, by Amy Reeder, Brandon Montclare, and Natacha Bustos, also has a somewhat cartoonish feel, though the characters are drawn in a relatively realistic fashion, and there is more three-dimensionality to the artwork. The lighthearted tone is due in part to the bright colors, which we can attribute to the work of the inkers, among other factors. This article, however, will focus on the impact of the line art.

Another tool that artists use to help advance the story is the use of backgrounds. The background does more than just set the scene – though that is one of its primary functions. The background can also help the action of a story flow more smoothly. For example, if Character A is going to hit Character B in the face with a pie, that pie needs to be seen in the background before Character A decides to use it. Perhaps the scene unfolds in a kitchen. The two characters argue for a few panels – with the pie sitting in the background but in plain view on a table next to them – before Character A snatches the pie up and throws it at Character B. If artists did not give care and attention to the objects in the background, this kind of natural flow of action would not be possible. Character A cannot suddenly grab a pie out of nowhere.

Art by Natacha Bustos from *Moon Girl and Devil Dinosaur* #1 (2015).

It's true that the writer might be the one to specify in the script which objects should be seen in the background. But this is sometimes the decision of the artist, as well. And even when it is a decision made by the writer, it is up to the artist to execute it in a way that will be easily comprehended by the reader.

The lack of a background can also be a powerful artistic statement. We will sometimes see a page in a comic in which the first few panels include a detailed background, in order to set the scene, and these panels will be followed by another panel in which the backdrop is completely black, for example. Since the setting has been established in earlier panels, this can be done without leaving the reader confused as to where the action is taking place. And the effect often heightens the emotional impact of the panel. By removing the background, there is nothing to distract from a character's facial expressions or gestures, giving the moment more weight and emphasis than it would have otherwise.

Finally, one of the important ways that the artwork contributes to the story is through the visual representation of characters. As is the case in film and movies, the way that a character is visually presented is extremely important to that character's development. How characters dress and carry themselves are very important factors that help the reader develop an idea of who those characters are.

And even more than that, the way that an artist represents a character's experience of emotional moments can do as much to develop that character as dialog or internal narration. A well executed facial expression, poignant body language, even a close shot of a character's eyes, can all tell us as much about what that character is experiencing as what's written on the page, and often more.

As the writer Neil Gaiman has pointed out, one of the advantages of the comic book medium is that it allows for story beats in which nothing is said. This cannot be done in a novel. Comics can feature extremely powerful panels revealing a character's emotional reaction to events, for example, without a single word being written. There is no equivalent to this in novel writing. Far from merely being an illustration of dialog or action, we can now see that the artwork itself is pivotal in developing the story and characters.

As noted above, there are some who believe that the artwork is in some ways secondary to the storytelling. By the same token, there are others who assume that the writer merely crafts the words in the dialog balloons, while the heavy lifting is done by the artist. Both beliefs are fallacies. The reality is that the writer and the artist – not to mention the inker, letterer, and editor – work together to tell the story. It is often said that in comics, writing the script is the equivalent of writing a screenplay, and creating the artwork is comparable to directing. This collaboration is what makes comics such a fascinating medium, and makes the end result more than just the sum of its parts.

What is Inking in Comics and How Does It Affect Your Aesthetic Reading Experience?

By Ben Towle

"That looks like a comic book drawing!" When someone makes a statement like this, what they're most likely responding to are the black outlines that make up a comics drawing – the inking. To the lay person, it is a comic's inked contour lines that really make comic art recognizable as comic art – more so than the abstract formal properties you may be used to thinking about ("Juxtaposed pictorial and other images in deliberate sequence...") if you study or write about comics. The practice of drawing comics with black outlines arose historically for practical reasons – in order to make drawn artwork suitable for mechanical reproduction – but it's become one of the main stylistic hallmarks of the art form.

The Mona Lisa, by Leonardo da Vinci (right), and a 1993 drawn/inked Mona Lisa by Scott McCloud (left).

Some cartoonists ink their own work. Some comics have a separate penciller and inker. Some recent comics even skip traditional inking all together, opting to darken pencil lines digitally. Whatever the case, the choice of inking tools, inking styles, and of course the skill of the inker can have a profound effect on what a finished comic looks like and how you experience it when reading.

Let's take a look at the first scenario: comics with a separate penciller and inker. This tends to be the norm with serialized monthly comics. It's a system driven by the need to produce an issue's worth of finished pages every month. It also, though, makes evaluating the inking difficult because as a reader you have no way to determine exactly how much of what you see on the page is directly attributable to the inker. A comic is first penciled, then inked. Once the ink is applied, the underlying pencil is erased, leaving just the ink. Without access to the original penciled pages (referred to as "the pencils") you have no way to discern exactly what role the inker of such a comic played.

Once you get familiar with a given penciller, though, and begin to see their work inked by different people, you'll begin to see the effects different inkers have and you'll discover that you respond differently to different styles of inking.

A good case study for this is cartoonist Jack Kirby. He was inked by a large number of different people over the course of his career and – quite unusually – there are readily available photocopy images of his pre-inked penciled pages. Head to the Kirby Museum's website (www.kirbymuseum.org) and look at single pages of Kirby's pencils and then the same page inked. Also: look at Kirby's art from the same period as inked by different inkers. Compare, for example, a Kirby Fantastic Four page inked by Vince Colletta with one inked by Joe Sinnott. You'll see a fairly radical difference.

A final consideration is how much leeway is implicitly given to the inker by the penciller in terms of how finished the pencils are. In some cases, the penciller may supply work with the expectation that the inker will add textures and details that may not be present in the pencils. In other cases, the penciller will supply highly detailed pencils that do not require this sort of work from the inker. Pages of the former sort are known as "loose" pencils; pages of the latter are referred to as "tight" pencils. In situations where the pencils are extremely loose and require substantial drafting work from the inker, the artists are sometimes credited for "roughs" and "finishes," rather than pencils and inks.

Example of tight pencils. Art Adams detail from *Ultimate Comics X* (2012).

Example of roughs. Steve Ditko detail from *Return of the Skyman* #1 (1987).

Outside the realm of monthly serialized comics, comics artwork – penciling, inking, and often lettering and coloring as well – tends to be executed by a single person, usually referred to as the "cartoonist" – or simply "artist." This situation obviously is much more straightforward as to what work is being done by whom, but ultimately in either case (separate artist and inker vs. single cartoonist) what you as a writer or critic will be responding to are the images on the page. And whether the ink is applied as a part of a multi-person process or by one individual artist, the decisions made at the inking stage greatly affect the appearance of the final artwork and how you respond to it.

Here are a few things to look for and consider as you evaluate a comic's inking:

Line weight – Line weight refers to the actual thickness of the ink lines and is a reflection of both the artist's style and of their inking tool choices they make. There is a general (but certainly not absolute) divergence between American and European inking line weights. Historically European comics have favored the "Ligne Claire," or clear line style, developed by Tintin cartoonist Hergé. One of the hallmarks of this style is the use of a thin line weight with very little line weight variation – meaning the line weight is consistently thin, with the artist not substantially varying the line thickness via pressure applied to the inking tool.

Hergé panel detail from *The Red Sea Sharks* (1958).

American comics, by contrast, have tended to favor a heavier and more variable line weight – often achieved by inking with a brush rather than a nib. Much of the look associated with classic American superhero comics is attributable to use of these heavy, variable ink lines.

Alex Schomburg cover detail from *The Black Terror* #6 (1944).

Manga tends to inhabit a middle ground: It's almost always inked with a nib, but tends to have more line variation/weight than a comic done in the European clear line style.

Spot blacks – Spot blacks are areas of solid black. Sometimes the peciller will indicate where these are to be added with an "x" on the penciled pages – you may have seen this if you've seen original comics art on display at a gallery or museum; other times the inker may have some discretion as to where to apply these areas. Whatever the case, the amount of solid black has a significant effect on the overall look and tone of a page. Think about how different these samples look compared to the *ligne claire* example above.

Right: Mike Mignola cover detail from *Hellboy: Wake the Devil* #4 (1996).

Look at the work of artists known for their effective use of spot blacks (Alex Toth, Mike Mignola, and John Paul Leon are examples) and compare them to artists who use spot blacks sparingly.

Black to white transitions – There are several ways to use ink to indicate a transition from an area of dark to area of light. This is often done in conjunction with an imagined light source in the scene in order to describe the volumes of the objects on the page. One prominent technique, especially in classic American superhero comics, is feathering. With feathering, the inker uses line weight variation to form a series of "teeth" that gradually expand into an area of spot black.

Charles Burns panel detail from *Black Hole* (2005).

Another common technique is hatching and/or cross-hatching. With cross-hatching, the artist uses a series of intersecting lines to create a gradient effect that goes from black to white. Hatching is a similar technique, but using parallel lines.

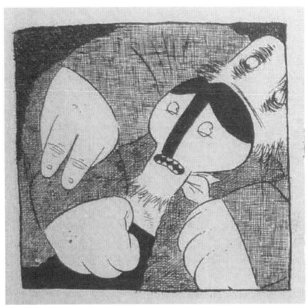

Example of crosshatching. Chris Wright panel detail from *Blacklung* (2012).

Example of hatching. Eric Orchard illustration detail (2012).

"Playing nicely" with color – In a black and white comic, the inking can wind up doing a lot more of the work of visually describing and object than in comics where color is also available to that end. Consequently, heavily hatched or crosshatched inking is most often seen in black and white artwork. In this situation, the hatching is being used to describe the volumes of objects, whereas with a colored comic the color itself can be used to model forms. A great side-by-side example of this is Peter Bagge's comic series, HATE, which switched from black and white to color. Note how the inking has changed to accommodate color.

Panels from early vs. late *Hate*.

Other techniques – A cartoonist or inker has myriad techniques at hand beyond basic outlining. Dry brush (applying the ink with a nearly-dry brush) can create a loose, expressionistic effect, for example.

Craig Thompson panel detail from *Blankets* (2003).

Ink washes – a diluted solution of ink in water – are sometimes applied over line art to provide additional values.

Gabriel Hardman panel detail from *Invisible Republic* (2015).

Sometimes traditional inking may not even be employed at all. Frank Quitely, for example, often darkens his pencils digitally rather than inking over them, trusting the colorist to play a larger role in some of the visual tasks usually performed by the inking.

Whatever the techniques employed by the artist, what is of course most important is the effect those techniques have on the overall appearance of the page.

Overly thin and uniform inking can sometimes give work a wispy, insubstantial look. Complex inking with heavy cross-hatching can yield a muddled, confusing look when used in conjunction with highly rendered color. Poor line width choices can fail to establish a believable visual space with depth of field. A profusion of washes, dry brush, and splatters in lieu of sufficient traditional contour outlines can fail to properly delineate and separate objects. Poorly placed spot blacks can render a scene or figure unrecognizable.

Yet, all these techniques – uniform line weight, heavy variable line weight, hatching and crosshatching. spot blacks – employed well can make a comics page a thing of true beauty.

When you look at a page of comics art, consider the inking. What if the artist had made different choices? Would thicker line-work improve or diminish the page aesthetically? What about thinner? More line weight variation or less? Feathering instead of hatching? Cross-hatching instead of feathering?

These inking choices are not arbitrary and they have a tremendous effect on the overall aesthetic appeal of a comic. The practice of drawing comics with black outlines may be a historical artifact of bygone printing practices, but it's come to be one of comics' most recognizable features – and to anyone tasked with evaluating a comic, it's an important aspect of the comics-making process to understand and to be able to evaluate.

Inking, the Invisible Art

by Harry Candelario and William Allred

Inking is an integral part of the comics creation process, but the art of inking is not well understood by readers, reviewers, or critics. Therefore, little, if any, attention is given to the contributions that inkers make to the published story. This attitude must change as inkers are an essential member of the art team. Fundamentally, inkers are responsible for the look of the finished artwork and must also be skilled artists themselves to properly interpret the intentions of the pencil artist. Contrary to what many believe, interpret is the proper term here. If inking were merely tracing, then every inker would produce the same finished art in conjunction with a particular penciller. Obviously, this is not the case.

Inking developed due to the requirements of the early printing processes. At the dawn of the comics medium, printing would not reproduce pencil artwork because it was too light. Thus, the lines had to be darkened, and the art of inking was born.

At this point, a brief discussion about the traditional roles in the comics creation process would probably be helpful. Historically, a writer would generate a script which contains the plot and dialogue for each panel of the finished story. This would then be handed to a pencil artist, or penciller. The penciller is responsible for translating the script into art. Pencillers "show" the story. They control the pacing, composition, and camera angles. They set the tone and mood of the story, whether it's a noir detective drama, a tender romance, a lush tale of sword and sorcery, or a stainless steel superhero comic. The next step in the comics assembly line is the inker, or ink artist. An in-depth discussion of this role will commence shortly. Once the inker completed the finished artwork, the colorist would take over, assuming, of course, that the finished product is a color comic. And finally, the letterer would add dialogue and captions and perform many of the post-production and pre-print tasks.

Since most readers and critics are not intimately familiar with the comics production process, they do not realize that most pencil artwork looks flat. This is not necessarily a bad thing. The penciller cannot spend time tweaking every single line of the artwork as this would greatly slow the process down. This is where the inker comes in. An inker's job is to enhance, to embellish, and to add depth and dimension to the pencil art through the use of thick and thin lines. This is accomplished through the use of various tools such as pens, magic markers and brushes. There are other tools that some inkers use, such as straight edge rulers, French curves, circle and oval templates, and a variety of other tools.

An inker has to plan most, if not the whole piece, before he or she ever puts pen to paper. This involves figuring out where to use thick or thin ink lines, where to crosshatch, which is shading with intersecting parallel lines, and where to simply fill in an area with black ink or some type of tonal wash, which is simply watered-down ink to make it gray. A seasoned inker can take good pencil art and make it great. Unfortunately, the power to improve does not exist without the power to damage or destroy. As many comics published over the preceding decades can attest, a bad or inexperienced inker can ruin the finest pencil artwork and make it unrecognizable.

Additionally, an inexperienced inker can make the work suffer by not fully understanding what the penciller intended. He or she may not yet understand how to create the depth or the texture required. Many novice inkers might even try to overpower the pencil art for several reasons. They might arrogantly think that they are actually improving or fixing the artwork, or they might be more concerned with establishing a name for themselves in the industry than with properly interpreting the penciller's artwork. They might also be trying to emulate their favorite artist, but their inexperience has not yet equipped them to understand the underlying reasons their favorite artist made the artistic choices that he or she made. Ultimately, it could simply be that the novice inker has not yet fully mastered his or her chosen craft and in doing so has failed in one or more of the four important functions of the inker which are 1) identifiability of the penciller, 2) the consistency of the finished artwork, 3) backgrounds, and 4) depth of the finished artwork. A brief discussion of each of these attributes follows.

When discussing the process of giving the art depth, one cannot avoid mentioning the artist Wally Wood (1927-1981). Wood was a consummate master at creating depth. He accomplished this through the use of large dark shapes in the foreground and fine line drawings pointed towards the back of the panel. Or, he achieved a similar effect by doing the exact opposite, fine details in the foreground of the panel and silhouettes in the background. Another tactic Wood employed was to utilize negative space, which is using the space around and between artwork, to create an optical illusion for the reader's eye. Wood also used zip-a-tone, a pre-printed, transparent sheet of patterns created with either black or white dots or lines. These sheets were cut out and applied to artwork to create different levels of grays in the panel. Any of these varying strategies were applied to the art with the goal of providing depth. Wood influenced generations of comic artists. In fact, it would be nearly impossible to find an inker today that has not been influenced by Wally Wood, whether he or she is aware of it or not.

Creating depth in comic art obviously takes skill, but it also takes intelligence. Depth is not created by simply inking in all the details in the background, regardless of whether it is a cityscape, a forest, or even a giant, diabolical super-computer. Inking is also about what to leave out. The inker needs to be aware of what the focus needs to be, but also what can be minimized. The same applies to characters. Simply giving all the characters in a panel the same amount of detail can and will render the art flat. Good, experienced inkers create depth within the art almost automatically.

Accomplished inkers know what to put in and what to leave out. Their experience has taught them what will be visible in the printed art and what would otherwise be wasted effort. As it would be extremely difficult to find two pencillers who draw identically, the same holds true for inkers. No two inkers think alike or even use the same tools. Each of them interprets depth, weight, light and shadow, and texture in completely different ways.

All of these inkers enhance the pencil art. They do not attempt to overpower the original pencil art and obscure the identity and style of the original penciller. Tim Townsend, for example, accomplishes this goal masterfully when he inks highly stylized artists like Joe Madureira or Chris Bachalo. Even after Townsend inks pencils from these different artists, the identity of the penciller is still obvious.

With the above as a framework and guide, the process of evaluating the inking on a particular story becomes much simpler. The first step in this assessment is the most important, and it involves story. The type of story being told by the pencil art must be determined. For example, a romance story would not look right if it were inked in a gritty, post-apocalyptic style, while the inverse is also true. A dark and gritty noir story would be rendered nearly unreadable if it were inked like a romance story.

Assuming that the inker has chosen the proper genre style in inking the story, determining the quality of the inking depends upon: (1) identifiability of the penciller, (2) the consistency of the finished artwork, (3) backgrounds, and (4) depth of the finished artwork. A brief discussion of each of these attributes follows.

Identifiability of the penciller is paramount, and an inker that continually obscures the identity of the pencil artist would quickly see a negative impact on his or her career. There are, however, two very specific situations where this obscuration is not only acceptable, but expected. The first would happen when the inker is working over loose pencils or breakdowns. Loose pencils or breakdowns are pencil artwork that simply is not complete. This is rarely done, but when it is, it typically involves an extremely experienced inker paired with a penciller who simply sets the pacing of the story. Everything else is up to the inker. A few inkers that excel in just such a scenario are Bob McLeod, Tom Palmer, and Rudy Nebres. The second situation where obscuring the identity of the penciller would be acceptable involves a neophyte penciller, one that is not well-versed in the rules of comics storytelling. Pairing this artist with an experienced inker would allow the inker to teach the the penciller the essential skills required of a penciller. Once this penciller gains the necessary knowledge and skills, then an inker would no longer allow his or her inking to overpower the penciller's art.

As a quick aside, there are some pencillers that are such accomplished artists that they are their own best inkers. Artists such as Neal Adams, Arthur Adams, Walter Simonson, Adam Hughes, Ed Benes, Mike Deodato, Bill Sienkiewicz, Todd McFarlane, and Mark Texiera have all worked successfully with other inkers, but there is something magical that occurs when they ink their own work.

Consistency of the finished art is the second barometer of good inking. An example of inconsistent finished art would contain meticulously inked panels or pages and rushed or sloppy inking on other panels or pages. Obviously, every artist wants to produce the best art possible, but meeting unrealistic deadlines can make any artist look bad or rushed. Experience has taught seasoned inkers how to deal with this situation, though. These inkers are intimately aware of the amount of time a possible job will take. This, of course, varies from inker to inker. Some can ink two pages a day or more, while others can only ink one page a day or less. It all depends upon the inker.

Backgrounds are an easy indicator, and not having the backgrounds done properly can be a major problem for the story. Having beautifully inked foreground characters and items in a panel or on a page while ignoring or rushing the background elements can bring the believability of the story to a grinding halt. Some inkers hire background assistants to help with this aspect of inking. In fact, many established inkers started out as background artists. They would start out by taking care of the tedious tasks like filling in black areas and ruling straight lines. As they gained experience, they would then begin inking the complete background.

Finally, the depth of the finished art is another important indicator. A page or panel that looks flat harms the story. As was mentioned earlier, pencil artwork has a tendency to look flat. The inker's job is to make the reader's eye flow to where it is required within the art. This involves differentiating between the foreground, middleground, and background. Inkers accomplish this by varying line widths. No professional inker worth his or her salt would ever hand in a finished page that looks flat. Inking the entire panel with the same line thickness, whether it's the foreground or background is a sin that no inker should ever commit.

At its core, inking is an additive process. Because it is so misunderstood, though, critics rarely touch upon the contribution inking makes to the finished art. Thus, they devalue its importance to the look of the finished art and, by extension, its impact upon the story. Inkers must be expert artists themselves to add the correct attributes to the finished art that serve the story. As such, inkers commonly include additional details to the page that enhances the pencil art. And as with each of the other roles within the comics creative process, inking must be evaluated on its contribution to the story. Frank Miller's artwork for *The Dark Knight Returns* would simply not look the same without the gritty inking of Klaus Janson. Bryan Hitch's artwork for *The Authority* would also look completely different without the slick inks of Paul Neary.

An Example of Brush Inking

The cover to *Legion of Super-Heroes* #70. Art by Alan Davis (penciller) and Mark Farmer (inker). From the collection of Miki Annamanthadoo

An Example of Pen Inking

Page 22 of *Aquaman* #15 by Paul Pelletier (pencils) and Art Thibert (inks).

An Example of Brush & Pen Inking

Page 14 of *Quasar* #39 by Steve Lightle (pencils) and Harry Candelario (inks).

Examples of Finishes

Page 1 of *Conan the Barbarian* #122 by John Buscema (breakdowns) and Bob McLeod (finishes).

Page 6 of *Conan the Barbarian* #122 by John Buscema (breakdowns) and Bob McLeod (finishes).

Understanding the Role of the Colorist

by Fraser Coffeen

The colorist stands tall as one of the vital, yet oft overlooked members of a comic book's creative team. It is the colorist who gives life to the art, adding depth and tone, and guiding readers through the page. Consider what a comic would be like without a colorist — what Superman would be like without his striking blue suit and red cape, or the Joker without his red lipped smile. A good colorist can bring new vitality to a piece, and understanding that work is key to appreciating what makes comics the unique artform we all love.

To understand coloring in comics, it is important to first know something of the history of the comic coloring process, as the technical limitations these artists have faced over the years greatly impact their work. In the early days of comics, colors were created by mixing only three colors together — cyan, magenta, and yellow (add in black and you have what is known as the CMYK color model). The colors were placed on screens and could then be mixed together in various combinations and at 25%, 50%, or 100% strength. These combinations left colorists with a limited palette of just 64 available colors.

This range of colors was further compromised by the quality of paper used. Cheap paper did not reproduce color well, making the difference between a purple with 25% red and a purple with 50% red virtually indistinguishable. The end result was, in practice, an even more reduced palette of closer to just 30 colors (this was especially true of DC Comics in the 1970s, which used very low quality paper).

This all changed in the late 1980s with the introduction of digital coloring. The American print of Japan's *Akira* is widely credited as the first major publication to use computers to color, and the effects on coloring are obvious and immediate. Colorists were no longer limited by the printing process and could use a vastly wider range of colors, textures, and effects. Perhaps too many in fact, as many comics of the early 1990s used every new digital trick available, frequently to the detriment of the story (as we will see in our discussion of focal points).

Today, digital is the industry standard, though there are of course those who prefer different methods. In our age of appreciation for all things retro, some modern colorists choose to intentionally limit their palettes to recreate the classic feel, creating a connection between their newer work and the classics – check out the work from Lauren Affe on the series *Five Ghosts* for a great example.

Ultimately, knowing when a comic was made and what was possible at that time is important in understanding that particular colorist's work.

The basics of comic coloring begin from the same point as numerous other visual arts – color theory. Entire books are written on this subject, so an examination of it here can only be at a surface level, but there are certain elements that are particularly relevant to the comic colorist.

Chief among these is the idea of contrasting and complementary colors. Contrasting colors are those that stand in stark contrast to each other. Pair them together and they draw the eye of the audience, creating visual interest and a sense of excitement. The most obvious and basic example of contrasting colors is of course black and white, and those comics that choose to stay in black and white make use of these contrasts to draw out their artwork. More on contrast and its relationship to the artist's work later.

Complementary colors are those that stand on opposite sides from each other on the color wheel. In the case of the three primary colors (red, blue, yellow), the complementary color is created by mixing together the other two primaries. So red complements green (there's a reason those are the official Christmas colors), blue complements orange, and yellow complements purple. When paired together, complementary colors bring out the brightness in each other, making for a more striking and visually bold look that creates a sense of excitement and energy.

Also important is the idea of warm and cool colors. Warm colors (oranges, reds, yellows) bring associations with sunlight and heat. They are colors used to stimulate the reader's visual sense. They also look like they are advancing, so create a sense of popping off the page. When a colorist adds these warm colors to an explosion, he brings the explosion across the page. Consider the predominantly red upper body of Spider-Man – when he swings forward, leading with his head and upper body, the red gives a feeling of excitement as if he is coming straight through the page towards you. (Spider-Man artists and colorists often make this effect even more pronounced by having one of his red hands extended out towards the theoretical camera.)

By contrast, cool colors (blues, greens) are associated with water and sky. They are soothing, calming, relaxing, and they help an image recede into the page. Because of this, while there are a fair number of comic heroes dressed entirely in warm colors (Iron Man and the Flash come to mind), virtually none are entirely cool. Those who do have a large amount of cool coloring will typically have a warm accent to give that excitement – think of the mostly blue Captain America with his striking red shield hurled at villains and readers with regularity. One notable exception is the entirely cool colored Batman. But of course, he is designed as a hero of the night, made to recede and hide in the shadows. The cool colors help him there, and create a powerful visual contrast when he is paired with his mainly warm colored and more dynamic boy wonder Robin. (For my money, this lack of contrast is partly why the more modern take on a "dark" Robin has never gained much mainstream recognition.)

Beyond just warm and cool, different colors are associated with certain emotions, which colorists use to their advantage. As any 9th grade student reading *The Great Gatsby* can tell you, green symbolizes greed; as a result, it is used more for villains such as the Joker, the Riddler, and Doctor Doom. Blue shows knowledge, power, and seriousness, resulting in the blue outfit for Batman and the blue skin of *X-Men*'s Beast. There are numerous psychological connotations to colors, and countless examples of their use in comics: the dark purple of Hulk's pants showing frustration and gloom; the bold yellow of Superman's logo indicating joy; the dark orange of *Fantastic Four*'s Thing showing his need for action. One of the best uses of these emotional appeals comes in the iconic image from *Watchmen* of a yellow smiley face button (bright yellow showing joy and freshness) splashed with a bold red drop of blood (rage and anger) – a perfect summary of the themes in Alan Moore's seminal work.

By bringing these aspects together – the warm and cool colors, and the emotional associations – colorists can use their choice of color to create tone. When done well, the chosen colors help establish a tone that places the reader in a specific emotional frame of mind simply by looking at the page. A great example of this comes from Frank Miller's *The Dark Knight Returns* where colorist Lynn Varley moved away from the brighter colors often associated with superheroes, replacing them predominantly with darker blues, greys, and browns. The result was a Gotham City that looked decrepit and dangerous – a look that has influenced nearly every rendition of Batman created since.

Varley's colors established the tone the instant you opened the book, adding to the emotional resonance and immersing the reader in Miller's world.

Key to the work of the colorist is the interplay between his work and the work of the artist. As acclaimed colorist Dave Stewart (*Hellboy*, *The Walking Dead*) explains: "I try to connect with the artist on what they think is appropriate under their art... to do what is appropriate for the project and mesh in the best possible way with the art."[1]

One of the chief ways art and color work together is through the use of contrast. Colorist K. Michael Russell (*Postal*, *Glitterbomb*) emphasized the importance of contrast by stating that, in the end, color doesn't truly matter – what matters is the contrast between colors.[2] As Russell explains it, while color can be used in the wide range of ways already outlined, one of the colorist's most important jobs does not rely on the specifics of color theory, and instead focuses on the use of color contrast to establish focus.

Each panel of a comic has (ideally) a central focus point – something that the artist wants to bring to the front of the reader's attention. Contrast is the colorist's tool to draw your attention to that focal point. If a panel is largely blue, a single splash of yellow will stand out, and wherever that yellow is found, that is where the reader's eye will go first. A good colorist can help subtly guide the reader to this point by bringing in colors different from the rest of the panel. This can also be extended from panel to panel across the page to help guide the reader through the work. The quick and easy way to accomplish this is by using a similar color just in a lighter gradient. However, this is not always effective; if the shades are too close together on the color spectrum, the result will be muddy and lack clarity – the goal of having the key image pop off the page will be lost. A talented colorist will draw on a variety of colors to create that contrast.

There is a fine balancing act at play in the creation of this point of focus. The process of adding coloring, shading, and texture is known as rendering, and

---

[1] Brothers, David. "The Art of Coloring: Making Comics with Dave Stewart [Interview]." *Comics Alliance*, 28 Sep. 2010, comicsalliance.com/dave-stewart-interview-coloring/. Accessed 12 Sep. 2016.

[2] Russell, K. Michael. "How NOT to Color Comics – Part 4 – Lack of value, contrast." *Comic Color*, 10 Aug. 2016, www.comiccolor.com/blog/2016/8/10/how-not-to-color-comics-part-4. Accessed 12 Sep. 2016.

it is through this rendering that the focus is created. However, as we already noted, the transition to digital coloring now provides the modern colorist with a wide arsenal of tools to use for rendering. The inexperienced colorist may find himself over-using these tools and ultimately over-rendering the image. The end result is a sloppy image that is too visually aggressive and lacks a clear focus. By attempting to make *everything* stand out, this colorist ends up making *nothing* stand out – once again, the focus is lost and the reader is left in the dark.

For the casual comic book reader, the work of the colorist is easy to take for granted and difficult to truly understand. It's an aspect of comics that seems so inherent to the form that we easily overlook it. But a true analysis of any comic should take into account the work of the colorist. As outlined above, when looking at color, a careful, analytical reading brings up the following questions:

1. When was the comic created and how did the colorist use the tools available at that time?
2. How has the colorist used color theory (warm vs. cool colors, complementary colors, emotional associations) to create tone?
3. How has the colorist used contrast to create a sense of clear focus?
4. Perhaps most importantly: how does the color work in connection with the art and script to create a cohesive vision?

Jordie Bellaire is an Eisner winning colorist known for her work on critically acclaimed series such as *Journey Into Mystery* and *Pretty Deadly*. She succinctly summarizes the work of her fellow colorists with this: "Colorists make or break a book."[3] The colorist represents often the final link in a chain of creators and visionaries responsible for a comic. From the author's initial idea, to the artist giving visual life to that idea, to the colorist giving that vision depth and meaning, the creation of a comic book involves an entire team, and the colorist, coming in at the end, forms an essential anchor to that team. And yet the colorist continues to be frequently overlooked. But that may be changing. Bellaire is an outspoken advocate for the importance of the colorist. She has challenged comic conventions that exclude colorists[4] and very publicly

---

[3] Bellaire, Jordie. "I'm mad as hell and I'm not gonna take it anymore." *jordiecolorsthings*, 2013, jordiecolorsthings.tumblr.com/post/41348547036/im-mad-as-hell-and-im-not-gonna-take-it. Accessed 12 Sep. 2016.
[4] Ibid.

questioned why Marvel does not include the colorist's name on their trade editions.[5] In 2013, her work inspired the creation of Colorist Appreciation Day.

Perhaps with colorists like Bellaire and many more at the wheel, and an acknowledgment of the particular artistry involved in this aspect of comic creation, the colorist of the future can gain the recognition deserved, not just as an interesting sidebar in the creation of a comic, but as a true artistic presence vital to that work's success – one who's work is essential in creating that marriage of image, text, and meaning distinct to comics.

---

[5] Sava, Oliver. "Comics colorist Jordie Bellaire on the art of coloring and stealing from the greats." The A.V. Club, 1 July 2016, www.avclub.com/article/comics-colorist-jordie-bellaire-art-coloring-and-s-238558. Accessed 12 Sep. 2016.

Three Styles of Color Narration

by Christopher McGunnigle

In *Understanding Comics* (1993), Scott McCloud outlines various effects produced by the use of color in graphic narrative. At the most basic level, he writes, "Colors objectify subjects. We become more aware of the physical form of objects than in black and white" (189). The whiteness of a volleyball, for example, would stand out on a blue background while the orange color of a redhead's hair would emphasize the difference between the character's hair and other facial features. McCloud adds more specific uses: "Colors could express a dominant mood. / Tones and modeling could add depth. / ... Color as sensation. Color as environment. / Color as color!" (190-91). One can also include color as narrative.

Although visual storytelling in graphic narrative is commonly dictated by the content of a panel, more specific artistic details like color can add to the effect of the panel image or panel sequence. A change in color scheme can suggest a change in story content and these color changes can form into a simplistic narrative based on interpretations of color symbolism. When panel content and color codes work together, the coherence of this color narrative is increased, enhancing the impact of image content, as well. Imagine, for example, that a volleyball game is illustrated for 12 panels all in shades of blue, then abruptly three panels are all in red. Blue is commonly associated with sadness or tranquility while red has come to symbolize activity, aggression, and intensity of emotion. When a long sequence of one color suddenly changes into another, an abrupt change in tone also suddenly occurs. Panel content can then fill in the specifics of what is going on, for example, a few boring rounds of warm-up and casually passing the ball is broken by a fierce spike that bloodies the nose of a player on the opposing team, who retaliates with a brutal serve, hitting the head of an opponent. While the image of a player's nose being bloodied by a volleyball is jarring in itself, the sudden shift in color and association of red with violence further aggravates the intensity of panel content. Being aware of the importance of color's narrative contributions can add to a critic's ability to analyze a comic, bringing forth a whole new level of understanding of the comic's visual design. Although a number of techniques can be used to construct a color narrative, three approaches are the most common: *alternation*, *masking*, and *insertion*.

Alternation

When panels or a sequence of panels alternate, they change color schemes to reflect panel content or add to it. Alternation can emphasize a change in scene, viewpoint, emotional expression, and an assortment of other shifts. The most classic example can be seen in *Watchmen* issue #3 (Nov 1983) with the convergence of two narratives. The first narrative is that of Dr. Manhattan's disastrous interview on a talk show, while the second has Dan Dreiberg and Sally Jupiter being accosted by hoodlums. The two narratives alternate every other panel with colorist John Higgins using different color schemes for each. Dr. Manhattan's narrative is primarily in shades of blue, white, and beige while Dreiberg and Jupiter's fight with the street hoodlums is depicted in hot colors of red, orange, and yellow (see fig. 1). Panel colors are emotional and elemental, with Dr. Manhattan's ethereal calm intellect in blue and white, and then the fire of red, yellow, and orange used in a scene of violence and conflict. Narrative also forms in the contrast between these colors, the fiery violence given more meaning when placed next to calmer colors.

Fig. 1. Alternation in panel color composition from soft tones to fire tones to display change in narrative subject, from page 13 of *Watchmen* #3 (Nov 1986) by John Higgins (colorist) and Dave Gibbons (artist).

Color change can also reflect a change in focus on character. When looking at a panel, what character is emphasized and what color scheme is associated with that character? In *Astro City* Vol. 3 #31 (Mar 2016), colorist Alex Sinclair depicts a confrontation between the Living Nightmare and the superheroic First Family in contrasting symbolic color schemes. For example, three panels have Julius Furst sitting in his technological blue, grey, and white headquarters, with the black body of the Living Nightmare growing in size each panel until he dominates the scene. Julius Furst retaliates, regaining the center of attention by grabbing a metallic gun from a similarly metallic weapon closet, with orange and yellow radiance glowing behind him (see fig. 2). At the level of the color narrative, blackness opposes shininess and illumination through a back-and-forth exchange of character focus, underscoring a thematic battle between darkness and light, good and evil.

Fig. 2. Alternation between blackness and illumination to display conflict between good and evil (and its ambiguity), from page 2 of *Astro City* Vol 3 #31 (Mar 2016) by Alex Sinclair (colorist) and Jesús Merino (artist).

Alternation does not need to occur in every other panel. A single color scheme can extend over several pages before changing. There is no set length for an alternation theme and different comic books will naturally use different paces. Dave Stewart in *Daytripper* varies his tempo, alternating anywhere from every half a page to every page and a half. For example, the first half page of *Daytripper* #1 (Feb 2010) gives a biopic-style narrative of three fictional historical characters in a dingy newspaper-colored whitish grey, while the next page and a half are in shades of reds showing the aftermath of a killing. The half-page segment that follows is of the main character, aspiring writer Brás de Oliva Domingos, reading a newspaper. Panels are colored with a wash of a sickly green before alternating to a light day-glo main narrative for another three pages to create a heightened sense of reality. In Dustin Nguyen's *Descender* #1, there is a shift from four pages of whites and blues to alternation of greys and blacks with blues and whites every half page. This alternation then leads into a six-page segment done almost entirely in blue following a doomsday robot attack, creating a tone of post-apocalyptic melancholic isolation.

Identifying a particular tempo of alternation can help define the aesthetic of an issue being analyzed. In many cases, the artistic merit of an individual page may not make sense until an alternating color theme is added. A segment that lasts for more than four or five pages thus risks disrupting the flow of the color narrative by lingering disproportionately on one scene. In these cases, a critic should dig deeper into reasons for such an extended color theme. *Daytripper*, for example, spends more time in its day-glo theme to establish it as the central narrative, while *Descender* needs a prolonged color segment to set up the isolation of the scene.

Masking

The color schemes used in extended segments of alternation, however, can lead to visual monotony. In order to reduce the risk of creating an unappealing panel image lost in an alternation scheme, *masking* introduces color narratives into the panel itself rather than a group of panels. According to McCloud, a technique in Japanese comic books is to create extensively detailed background settings while characters are kept overly simple. He writes, "This combination allows readers to *mask* themselves in a character and safely enter a sensually stimulating world" (43; emphasis added). Masking takes place when the artist leaves out details in order to allow the reader to "put on the mask of that character" to relate to them. Traditionally, masking is performed mainly by the line artist, not the color artist, but in approaching a comic book, a critic should feel free to consider how artistic techniques from one stage of comic book production can be applied to another. Masking can also occur where rather than details being left out, color emphasizes one aspect of the panel's visual narrative while de-emphasizing other components of the image. This contrast typically occurs between character and setting, but the masking effect can be seen anywhere where one color dominates or contrasts with another.

Fig 3. Making effect between a character and his background to demonstrate difference and alienation, from page 4 of *Sweet Tooth* Vol 1 #1 (Nov 2009) by José Villarrubia (colorist) and Jeff Lemire (artist).

The credits page to *Sweet Tooth* #1 (Nov 2001), for example, has multiple layers of masking. Colorist José Villarrubia visually distinguishes the main character, Gus, a boy-deer hybrid, from the forest in which he stands by dressing him in a red flannel shirt (see fig. 3). This difference is furthered by shading the woody backdrop in blue and black. Normally, a deer in the woods blends in naturally, but Gus' flannel marks him as different from the normal fauna of the forest. White snow in the foreground where Gus stands adds another level of masking to separate Gus from the forest, but this snow also sets up a contrast between Gus as representative of a weird post-apocalyptic manifestation of emerging new life and the snowy, hostile conditions in which he lives. Villarrubia similarly colors Gus' dying father, who represents the passing of the former world order, in shades of grey and white like dirty snow. When Gus and his father are juxtaposed or alternated, there is a visual disparity between the (un-natural) life conditions of Gus and the (un-natural) death conditions of his father (see fig. 4).

Fig 4. Masking effect distinguishing two characters through color scheme, emphasizing themes of life and decay, from page 6 of Sweet Tooth Vol 1 #1 (Nov 2009) by José Villarrubia (colorist) and Jeff Lemire (artist).

Masking can work to emphasize character over environment, or vice versa, as well as differentiating characters. A side effect of alternation is that this color technique immerses a character in a singular color scheme, effectively un-masking the relationship between character and environment so that neither stands out. For example, the extended use of blue in *Descender* creates such an un-masking effect, where the robot boy Tim-21 and his spaceship are nearly the same color (see fig. 5). Tim-21's creator Dr. Quon lives in a sci-fi world that ranges from bright to dull white, appearing sterile and monotonous. To counter this uniformity, Dr. Quon has black hair and dresses in a black suit, like ink on white paper. Captain Tesla, meanwhile, dresses almost entirely in a white uniform but her bright orange hair jumps out from her surroundings, visually competing with Quon's drab black outfit (see fig. 6). Tesla lives in the wild and imaginative world of *Descender*'s science-fiction – her white outfit represents her environment while her hair, its spectacle. Meanwhile, Quon is a fallen prodigy from the past who no longer produces technological wonders, seen in his achromatic masking. Within a single panel, the masking narrative establishes setting and character through color contrasts and insertion.

Fig. 5. Un-masking effect created by lack of contrast between character and background, denoting the character's homogeneity with his environment, from page 17 of *Descender* Vol 1 #1 (Mar 2015) by Dustin Nguyen.

Fig. 6. Masking effect distinguishing characters and displaying thematic personality through use of color, from page 24 of *Descender* Vol 1 #1 [Mar 2015] by Dustin Nguyen.

Insertion

With insertion, color functions as a rudimentary object formed by the geometric boundaries of color contrasts. McCloud writes, with color, "The world takes on the childhood reality of the playground and recalls a time when shapes preceded meaning. Oblong swing sets. Cylindrical jungle gyms. The wonder of things" (189). With insertion, visual elements are broken down into the individual shapes and colors that contribute to the visual design of the panel. How does a particular design element stand out in terms of its shape and color and control the reading of other elements? Does an individual shape of color control panel space? Do objects throughout the panel guide the eye of the reader? Can design elements be broken down into smaller shapes and colors or does a design element stand as a singular object? Narratives can also be created by how the reader reads and assembles the image in a panel.

Insertion uses colored shapes in a variety of approaches to assist narrative production – a mosaic of shapes, a singular piece, coordinating individual pieces, a controlling focal point, or a symbolic object, among others. The first page of *Descender* #1 has dozens of brightly and differently colored vehicles driving on vast highway ramparts or floating in the sky among pure and shining skyscrapers with green and red vegetation on their balconies. Focusing in on Dr. Quon's apartment, Nguyen colors it in whites and blues like a translucent screen, inserted with paintings and statues that stand out among the almost blinding translucency of his room. Closer shots of each item beg the question as to what they are, but these objects also guide the eye around each corner of the panel (see fig. 7 and 8).

Fig. 7. Insertion of color through use of objects that contrast with background color, guiding the reader's eyes throughout the panel and revealing character through artifact, from page 3 of *Descender* Vol 1 #1 (Mar 2015) by Dustin Nguyen.

Fig. 8. Insertion of color through use of objects that contrast with background color, guiding the reader's eyes throughout the panel and revealing character through artifact, from page 4 of *Descender* Vol 1 #1 (Mar 2015) by Dustin Nguyen.

In *Astro City* #31, Sinclair and artist Jesús Merino illustrate the Living Nightmare's black body with a fiery center composed of gradients of orange and yellow shaped like eyes and a mouth (see fig. 9). Literally, this is the Living Nightmare's face, but the insertion of color connects the Living Nightmare with the illumination found throughout the First Family's headquarters, marking the center of his shadowy evil with a brilliant heroic light.

Fig. 9. Insertion of color into a black figure to create a visual contrast effect, mixing the darkness of monstrosity with the illumination of heroism on page 6 of *Astro City* Vol 3 #31 (Mar 2016) by Alex Sinclair (colorist) and Jesús Merino (artist).

In some cases, abstract colored objects are inserted to call attention to aspects of a panel narrative. For example, in *Sweet Tooth* #2 (Dec 2009), Villarrubia inserts red circles throughout a fight scene as Jeppard defends himself and Gus from a band of masked attackers. Each circle spotlights an inflicted wound — one where Jeppard catches a spiked club with his hand and another where he catches a club in his armpit. Below this fight scene, an entire panel illustrated in red depicts a close-up of Jeppard slashing the throat of one of the attackers (see fig. 10). The red circles not only draw attention to these parts of the panel through the contrast with the panel's grey-tone color scheme but also emphasize the violence of the sequence with color symbolism.

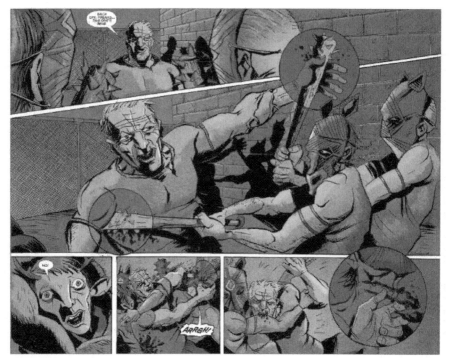

Fig. 10. Insertion of color to create visual emphasis to narrative details, from pages 17-18 of *Sweet Tooth* Vol 1 #2 (Dec 2009) by José Villarrubia (colorist) and Jeff Lemire (artist).

Conclusion

Graphic narrative is a medium that combines both words *and* images into a singular design, so when reviewing, analyzing, or criticizing a comic book, you have a responsibility of not only addressing problems and strength in storytelling but also in the visual presentation of that story. Acquiring a vocabulary that helps you focus on artistic techniques is a vital tool in critiquing comic book art. This chapter lays out different uses of color to construct a rudimentary narrative that adds to the story told by panel content and sequences. The essence of color narrative comes through contrast or change in color at three major levels. The first level is in alternation where panels are given different color schemes to emphasize differences in content. With masking, color contrast occurs between elements in panel. One can formulate color narratives based on infinitely microscopic variations of relationships so that each aspect of design presents its own form of narrative. Insertion, for example, shows how elements can be added to a panel to (re)center panel content and their narrative. At a deeper level, specific colors can express particularities of the narrative rather than just emphasizing changes – something down to earth, something violent, something dark and sinister. Combined with an analysis of panel content, an understanding of color narrative can add layer of meaning to a comic book narrative. Using these approaches will give you a good starting point in critiquing panel and cover art but also provide a first step or two in developing your own criteria of approach.

Bibliography

Higgins, John (c), Dave Gibbons (a), and Alan Moore (w). "The Judge of All the Earth." *Watchmen* Vol 1 #3 (Nov 1986), DC Comics.

McCloud, Scott. *Understanding Comics: The Invisible Art.* New York: HarperCollins, 1994.

Nguyen, Dustin (a), and Jeff Lemire (w). "Tin Stars: Part I." *Descender* Vol 1 #1 (Mar 2015), Image Comics.

Sinclair, Alex (c), Jesús Merino (a), and Kurt Busiek (w). "Nightmare Life." *Astro City* Vol 3 #31 (Mar 2016), DC Comics.

Stewart, Dave (c), Fábio Moon (w / a), and Gabriel Bá (w / a). "32." *Daytripper* Vol 1 #1 (Feb 2010), DC Comics.

Villarrubia, José (c), and Jeff Lemire (w / a). "Out of the Deep Woods Part One." *Sweet Tooth* Vol 1 #1 (Nov 2009), DC Comics.

---. "Out of the Deep Woods Part Two." *Sweet Tooth* Vol 1 #2 (Dec 2009), DC Comics.

How to Analyze Comic Lettering

by Suman Sigroha

One may be aware of the existence of a comic, either the shorter strips or the longer comic books or the still longer graphic novels. Generally, one reads these comics for amusement and escape that these fantasy worlds offer. For this same reason, many a times a comic is also supposed to be meant for young readers only, however, a close analysis of various elements of a comic reveal that this is certainly not the case. The current essay aims to make the comics more accessible to the non-academic reader analysts who would benefit from a better understanding of one of the important elements of the comics i.e. lettering and in this process make the case for the complexity of these otherwise apparently simple narratives. Understanding lettering would help make the reading of various comics or graphic novels like Batman, X-Men, Superman, Persepolis, Maus, Watchmen, or Tintin a richer experience.

Lettering: An Introduction

A panel of a comic strip many a times conveys more than a paragraph of a traditionally written text. The picture alone speaks volumes, but the presence or the absence of the text adds to this already speaking picture. Since, a comic is essentially a combination of images drawn by an artist and words written by the writer and conveyed by the letterer, the writer's and the letterer's roles are significant. Dialogue carries forward this longer narrative to its envisioned end and this is where the element of lettering comes in. Lettering refers to the written word (dialogue, symbols, signs, and balloons) and its various aspects that help enhance the meaning of the image and thus further the narration. The style and the size of the words used for lettering help the letterer communicate the intentions of the writer, with due emphasis, better to the readers. The style encompasses various elements of the words and lines used like font, format, size, and color, along with the usage of punctuation marks and various other symbols. These elements give meaning, add emphasis, reflect emotions and give voice to an otherwise mute picture, however expressive it may be. They add sound to an overwhelmingly visual experience. Additionally, the presence of lettering is contrasted by its absence in some panels and because of its utter lack it becomes as important to understand as any presence. The text that adds to the meaning being conveyed by the image perhaps expresses more if it is removed. The ensuing deafening silence some times proves more powerful than any noise made by the words.

Presences

The primary function of lettering in the comics is to represent a vital element of human experience – the sound. Because of its overwhelming presence in the world around, its presence is taken for granted. The letterer conveys speech and sounds, and the visual nature of the medium requires them to be made visual.

So how does the comic, an overwhelmingly visual form, illustrate these sounds to make them audible as well? How does it make the image perform this important act of speaking? The answer lies in the use of letters, words, symbols, signs and lines, accentuated by their style, size and thickness, reflected in the dialogue, the captions, the sound effects, and sometimes via the footnotes. While, dialogue takes the conversation forward and reveals the thoughts behind actions of a character, the captions are the more direct tools in the hands of the letterer. Thus, the letterer needs to combine these two disparate forms – words and images – in an organic whole for the comic to be read clearly and easily. Dialogue and captions need to be unobtrusive and carefully placed within the panels for the readers to engage with the comic in a comprehensive manner, hence the spacing and the font used are crucial while doing or understanding the lettering.

Dialogue

Dialogue is mostly placed in balloons that appear to emanate from the mouth of a character and which are drawn in different shapes and sizes. Their function is to draw a reader into the story by creating a sense of proximity to the characters, their thoughts and actions. The style used brings in a sense of immediacy for the readers, of being engaged with the action, perhaps *flying* with the Spiderman or *agonizing* over an intended action with the Batman. Generally, the smooth oval balloons are meant for a normal conversation or to convey a thought. The latter are called thought balloons and are the more indirect means of transmitting information to the readers. Thought balloons allow the readers to eavesdrop on personal motivations of a character and their presence or relative absence has the effect of making a character appear either open, articulate and knowable or distant, mysterious and incomprehensible. The Batman becomes a brooding and enigmatic figure as soon as he wears the mask and the letterer refrains from giving the readers an insight into his contemplations. However, if used indiscriminately, they tend to question the intelligence of the readers by presenting all the information instead of leaving some things to the readers' imagination.

The other types of balloons basically conform to a loose oval or a circle that has zigzagged lines. Such balloons usually enclose mechanical voices, the ones coming from devices like radio, television, telephone, computer, loudspeaker, and so on. The balloons with curly lines or broken lines (given below) express innermost feelings and plans of the characters, a means of talking directly to the readers. These are also crude stylistic devices to convey the opinion of the writer.

One way to understand the significance of different dialogues is the line weight used in these dialogues as well as the thickness of the lines of the balloons. The thicker the line, the louder is the tone of the voice supposed to be. Usually, changes in the line weight are seen when the character is whispering, but otherwise, standard line weight is used. If the volume of the dialogue is to increase, the letterer either bold-faces the dialogue or increases the font size or adds CAPS (or a combination of these options).

Captions

Narrator's first person or third person voice talks to the readers through the captions. They are generally placed in the upper empty space in a panel, mostly enclosed within round edged rectangles or ovals. They may also be placed at the bottom or the sides according to the picture drawn for intended effect. Although not the same, these first person captions are the preferred internal narrative device that substitute dialogue or thought balloons many a times and articulate a character's thoughts as clearly as any dialogue does. The other types of captions, the open narrative captions, are placed on top in any panel and are a stylistic tool to carry the narrative further. Unlike the dialogue, these (being the author's voice) are generally more measured in tone and act as distancing tools by creating a disassociating effect from the immediate action. However, if the letterer is not careful, they may have the very opposite effect of what a comic generally aims for – intimacy. Footnotes are mostly used to explain either the terms used or associations made earlier during the course of the narrative and are the least used of the captions because of their intrusive nature.

Words in Action

A reader of a comic is not merely influenced by the balloons and their lines but also by the content of these balloons. The hand lettering of earlier times has now been replaced by computer fonts and thus words become much easier to add as well as clearer to read. Although, the former enhanced the engagement and hence the experience of a reader, it had its limitations as well. A missed letter or a punctuation mark could convey a totally different meaning to the one actually intended. Computers, by making the fonts clearer to read, help achieve the desired effect more forcefully. Coming to the actual words, normal text points to a normal conversation, bold-facing the text or underlining adds emphasis to it, capitalizing adds the dimension of loudness to the sound represented and italicizing tends to point towards a thought. Symbols, like a dollar sign or a hash ($, #), communicate the otherwise difficult to communicate emotions like greed, anger, frustration, etc. and the more their number, the greater the degree of emotion being conveyed. Since, the comics were supposed to be an expression of as well as means of achieving wish fulfillment fantasy, they were generally thought to be juvenile in nature, meant to cater to children or adolescents and hence, needed to be kept *clean* or free of curse words. Instead, the letterers used signs and symbols to express curses and profane language. Even though letterers are increasingly using the curse words (albeit in hyphenated or short forms), they are still conveyed through the more traditional means of signs and symbols (#@!&%, etc.). Other signs like exclamations and question marks were also frequently used to end sentences in dialogues. Although, earlier they were used to replace the period because of the difficulties of hand-lettering (a period may be easily missed or misread when written in a running hand), and have now been replaced by the more legible computer generated ones, they are still used to express excitement, speechlessness, wonder and amazement. Their repetition gives added emphasis to these emotions. One question mark makes an enquiry, two bewilderment, but an excess of !!! or ??? or a combination thereof ??!!, despite being intended for an increased effect, appears exaggerated, absurd and ludicrous.

Most of the letterers prefer to use black color for words not only for the sake of consistency of the narrative but also for its unobtrusiveness. It would appear distracting if different characters spoke in different colors, and by bringing attention to the words rather than to the voice they are meant to represent, otherwise meant to be an integral part of the image, would disrupt the act of reading the comic as a fluid whole.

At times, words appear without the accompanying images and act as images in their own rights. A blast can easily be represented by a capital, bold and huge **BOOM** surrounded by similarly bold thick zigzag lines, emerging out of the middle of a panel. The devastating effect that it aims for is not lost because of the missing images of destruction, it is rather enhanced by this gargantuan word obscuring everything else in that panel. And by doing so, it easily becomes the image that it replaced.

Absences

The focus so far has been on analyzing the presence of words in a comic, but what does it mean if there are no words in a panel or even a whole page? The lack of words expresses certain emotions more emphatically than any narrative caption or dialogue does. Such instances show the truth of the adage that a picture is worth a thousand words. An image of a wordless open mouth, contorted with fear or pain, screams out fear or pain louder than any balloon saying, "scream" or "aah" would ever do. Actually writing *scream* or *yell* would not only appear incongruous but also make it sound ridiculous. Letterers use words like *bam, boom, bang, thud, thump, crash, yeow, clack, ring, tring, whirr, gasp, slam, scratch,* and *zzz* to represent sounds. To show the intensity of these sounds, these words are either made capital and boldfaced or are accompanied by zigzag lines, and like other words used, the line weight or the size conveys their intensity. However, the force of the intended effect increases manifold if no sound effects are shown at all in those particular panels, even though they are preceded by an increasing crescendo of the babbling voices and succeeded by a representation of consequent reactions. Imagine a fight building up to its climax, with all the related sounds – *boom, bam, bang, ouch, yeow* – and suddenly the protagonist is hit by a bullet, the panels that had been following each other in quick succession, pause. The dramatic effect increases if all the surrounding noises are also muted, the slower panels wordlessly depict the slow fall. The readers do not see or hear anything except the soundless fall, the strength of the effect having been amplified by this profound silence. Thus, an absence of words and sounds speaks volumes. The letterer makes the readers pause, contemplate, mull over the supposed consequences before helping tide over the present crisis or plunging them into the next one.

Since, images without words also help involve the readers, hold their attention for longer spells at times and thus lengthen the experience, they tend to leave a more profound impact on the readers. At such times, the letterer requires a deeper engagement and erudition on part of the readers to understand these unspoken emotions, thoughts, ideas and plans. Even though the rendering of images, words and lines impart both personality and emotions to the characters (and by extension, to the comic), absences accentuate the visual as well as the aural aspects of the comics by making the readers pause and ponder, and think like and alongside these characters. As mentioned earlier, at other times, the reverse also happens; the panel consists of letters only and sometimes letters are placed between the panels in the gutter. These mostly refer to action taking place off-stage, beyond the purview of the current panel but which may have repercussions on the events happening in the subsequent panels. Again, the objective is to not only build up the curiosity and sustain the interest but also to achieve greater intensity of effect and consequent emotional reaction before the final catharsis.

Conclusion

Lettering is thus an integral element of comic writing and its proper understanding is crucial in comprehending the text as well as appreciating the act of writing/making a comic. This perception of the comic further augments the aesthetic experience that reading a comic generally is. The discerning reader clearly recognizes that the comic world is essentially a microcosm of the real world and reflects the real world political, economic, social and psychological experiences, ideologies and developments within the confines of its pages.

Bibliography:

Behler, Anne. "Getting Started with Graphic Novels: A Guide for the Beginner." Reference & User Services Quarterly, Vol. 46, No. 2, 2006, pp. 16-21.

Blake, Peter. "Lettering as Popular Art." RSA Journal, Vol. 139, No. 5419, 1991, pp. 448-454.

Dallacqua, Ashley K. "Exploring Literary Devices in Graphic Novels." Language Arts, Vol. 89, No. 6, 2012, pp. 365-378.

Drucker, Johanna. "Graphic Devices: Narration and Navigation." Narrative, Vol. 16, No. 2, 2008, pp. 121-139.

Eisner, Will. Comics and Sequential Art. Poorhouse Press, 2000.

Rennie, Paul. "Fat Faces All Around Lettering and the Festival Style." Twentieth Century Architecture, No. 5, 2001, pp. 108-116.

Williams, Rachel Marie-Crane. "Image, Text, and Story: Comics and Graphic Novels in the Classroom." Art Education, Vol. 61, No. 6, 2008, pp. 13-19.

"More than Words: Analyzing Typography and Lettering in Comics"

by Michael James Griffin II

In regards to the printed, written text, readers are often meant to understand the role of typography – the vehicle of language in written communication – *as the substance* that makes up the literary text but not *as the work of art*. Typography in the case of the printed novel is, thus, oddly enough, *invisible*, which is a classic hallmark of bookmaking and the act of reading. Readers are not meant to contemplate the type itself, but instead utilize that type to access the deeper meaning created by them. Consider Beatrice Warde's philosophy, noted typographer and bookmaker of the early 20th century, particularly her essay "The Crystal Goblet, or Printing Should Be Invisible" (1930): "the most important thing about printing is that it *conveys thought, ideas, images, from one mind to other minds*. [...] We may say, therefore, that printing may be delightful for many reasons, but that it is important, first and foremost, *as a means of doing something*. That is why it is mischievous to call any printed piece a work of art, especially fine art: because that would imply that its first purpose was to exist as an expression of beauty for its own sake and for the delectation of the senses" (13, emphasis mine). For Warde, typography is the invisible container, the crystal goblet, that holds together the "work of art."

Warde's understanding of typography, however, stands at odds with how readers analyze lettering in comics, which most vividly asks readers to consider the visual dimensions of the written word. When thinking about comics, a form which relies on the relationships among written and visual modes of communication, typography and lettering takes on that visual, or perhaps aesthetic, dimension in that it assimilates both the understanding of typography as described by Warde as well as how type can also serve as the foundation of the visual/visible art of comics.

Comics scholars Scott McCloud and Will Eisner locate the role of letterings in comics in two distinct places: in the written text and the visual image. In his definition of comics as the "juxtaposed pictorial and other images in deliberate sequence intended to convey information and/or to produce an aesthetic response in the viewer," Scott McCloud, in *Understanding Comics* (1993), conspicuously leaves out "written text" or "type" in lieu of "other images" (9). As detailed in his chapter on the Picture Plane, McCloud locates language, and thus consequently written text and the alphabet, as the ultimate abstraction of non-iconic images.[6] The justification of written language's placement in the Picture Plane is supported by Will Eisner's work in *Comics and Sequential Art* (1985): "Words are made up of letters. Letters are symbols that are devised out of images, which originate out of familiar forms, objects, postures and other recognizable phenomena" (8). For Eisner, and subsequently for many others cartoonists, lettering in comics has always contributed to the meaning of comics, whether through its deployment as written text or inspiration for graphic expression (8).[7]

What then should readers consider when analyzing lettering and typography in the comics form? To what extent should lettering fade into the background, or in contrast, when does the art of lettering become worthy of our readerly and critical attention? In what follows, I will start with a scheme to consider when analyzing lettering in comics before entering into a wider discussion about the relationship between typography and lettering that incorporates a brief history of lettering in comics to contextualize what might be of interest in regards to lettering to new comic book readers.

Scheme for Analyzing Lettering

The comic book letterer is the artist who takes the writer's script and adds the captions, dialogue, and various sound effects to the panels of interior art. While the job of lettering may be distinct from that of the illustrator and the author in large publishing houses, it is not always a job performed by other artists in either independent, creator-made comics.

---

[6] Scott McCloud's "Picture Plane" is a diagram that situates all genres, styles, and forms of graphic representation in relation to realism, abstraction, and iconic/language to discuss the breadth of comics' "visual vocabulary." McCloud uses this diagram to further his argument about the capacious nature of visual representation in comics.

[7] Figure 1. From Will Eisner's *Comics and Sequential Art: Principles and Practices from the Legendary Cartoonist*. Norton, 2008.

When thinking critically about how lettering is used in comics, readers, should ask how the presentation of the text changes the reading experience. To what end is lettering presented or displayed beyond simply for the delivery of dialogue? How do changes in color or font alter your ability to understand written text? What makes one style of presentation stand out for you? How might uniformity allow for an easier reading experience, making typography and lettering *invisible*? While these questions are not exhaustive, they do begin to isolate three distinct attributes of lettering readers can use to begin thinking critically about lettering: purpose, design/style, size/location.

Purpose

When considering lettering in the comics, we can divide its function between narrative, world-building, and the paratextual.

The narrative component of lettering – the creators' use of narrative voice, dialogue, sound effects, and captions – is by far its most predominant use. Obviously, this type of written text is best interpreted most often using analysis or critical schemes used in literary analysis. While I will not harp on any particular critical school or theory, readers may want to consider the relationship between written text and image that is a hallmark of comics. Undoubtedly the most unique inclusion of a letterer's work in comics would be the illustration of sound effects because this type of written text is always visually distinct from the dialogue/narrative that predominantly fills comics. From the "BUDDA, BUDDA, BUDDA" of machine-gun bullets in *Captain America* (2005, Letterer: VC's Randy Gentile) to the repeated "SKREE" of the bats in Frank Miller and Klaus Janson's *Batman: The Dark Knight* (1986, Letterer: John Costanza), sound effects in comics have a style unto themselves. As critical readers of comics, we can start by asking ourselves: how do these sound effects impact how we experience reading the story? We might also consider how the aesthetic and playful rendering of this multimodal device asks readers to utilize their own imagination at the intersection of the visual and the verbal.

The secondary purpose for which lettering may be used is in a comics' world-building, by which I mean the way in which the creator uses written text to breathe life into the world inhabited by his characters. We see this usage in comics as diverse as Alan Moore and Dave Gibbon's *Watchmen* (1987, Letterer: Dave Gibbons) with its metropolitan street signs, punk rock posters, and advertisements for Adrian Viedt's corporate products to the perpetual deployment of newspaper headlines in the Marvel universe comics, most notably *The Daily Bugle*, in titles from *The Pulse* to *Amazing Spider-Man*. While this use of lettering need not always be crafted specifically by the comics' letterer, it does further a reader's understanding of how written text can be used to elaborate or enhance the world depicted in comics.

Paratextuality refers to the way in which publishing features such as a title, table of contexts, epigraphs, or chapter titles can alter the reading experience. Paratextual features, much like sound effects, carry their own distinct style. To better contextualize how paratextuality impacts lettering, consider Karin Kukkonen's discussion of superhero comics: "superhero comics have developed a very detailed encyclopedia of costumes and visual attributes, an iconography that provides shortcuts into readers' knowledge structures, enabling readers to keep different character versions distinct and connect them to their original storyworlds" (157-158). While I will discuss this concept further below, what Kukkonen's idea suggests is how the similar, distinct devices provide information that grounds a reader within a comic world. For instance, the superhero icons and costumes of characters are mirrored in the written text through the title's logos, font choices, and more. Building on this concept, readers can see how an artistic use of paratextual features enhance both the narrative and world-building elements of a comic; take for instance the use of the title in DC's New 52 *The Flash* (2011-2017), in which each rendering of the title, "The Flash," is uniquely drawn and lettered by the creators, artist Francis Manapul and letterer Wes Abbot.

Design/Style

As a critical reader of comics, the unique design and style of lettering may be of greater importance than necessarily how written text is used for narrative purposes. From color to font choice, how written text is designed by the letterer can transform the reading experience, as it shapes and guides the reading experience. While in color comics black is the standard color for narrative text, sound effects are often rendered in colors and fonts completely different from the narrative to stand out and/or to jar the attention of readers.

Let's return to Kukkonen's idea about costumes, storyworlds, and visual vocabulary. Given that interpretation of how comics use visual language, consider particularly how in superhero comics of the last 20 or so years lettering also take on this same dimension. By that I mean, now specific characters have their own fonts, colors, and styles to denote their written speech: the red and yellow, thin, mechanical dialogue of Marvel's Tony Stark or the Medieval-inspired, rounded and robust lettering of Marvel's Thor. This style even transcends just written text to include the design of word balloons and dialogue boxes, which have fills and borders that set these features apart from traditional text boxes. This dimension of specialized text boxes is not limited to just superhero comics, though it does arise most prominently in that genre. Two notable outliers are Neil Gaiman's *Sandman*, where many different characters, particularly those mythological ones, are given their own lettering theme and iconicity and Brian K. Vaughn and Fiona Staples's *Saga* (2012-ongoing), in which the main characters each have their own distinct fonts and colors to denote the speaker.

Two final concerns for design are logos and titles in comic books. Indeed, letterers are most famously known for their (re-)branding of classic comic books and comic book characters because of the focus put on logos, which help to market a book. From readability to appropriateness, a logo's design has the ability to grab the attention of a potential reader, just as titles are meant to "capture the essence of the story."[8] Whereas lettering guidebooks note the importance of originality, for new critics of comic books what we should look for most in logos, titles, and story titles is how those lettering tasks serve as a shorthand for the much larger work done by the visual content of the comic book.

Size & Location

While in one-way size is related to design and style, I set this feature of lettering apart because it is worth noting that size is not always reliant upon design but upon the amount of space on the page left "open" by the illustrator. As your eyes navigate the comics page, it's worth noting how dialogue, narrative, and the like pull your eyes across visual images in the comic. Often, narrative or editorial text boxes featured above panels, while dialogue is contained within panels or word balloons that are superimposed over visual content. A letterer's job may be to decide the placement of these textual devices depending on illustrator, publisher, or writer.[9]

Nevertheless, when thinking about the size and location of panels, readers should always approach analyzing this component with a critical understanding

---

[8] Chiarello and Klein 106; Starkings and Rochell 37.
[9] Chiarello and Klein 101-103.

of how written text and visual image work together. Readers should ask how the text's placement effects reading visual images. For instance, when dialogue boxes float above the talking heads of characters, is that distracting? How might that better serve the illustrations as opposed to the story? Or when text boxes flow down and up pages over characters, the setting, and multiple panels, does it disrupt your understanding of how the written text is presented visually, or inversely does it guide your reading experience? The location of lettering within panels can pull the eyes in certain directions. And while these questions may highlight a reader's response to lettering, they also underscore the technical nature of lettering in comics from the ways in which word balloons and textboxes interact with art to house styles regarding the generally accepted amount of words allotted to text boxes – 25-35 words per balloon, 200 words per page.

A key component of size to consider is fill, which refers to the amount of space *filled* within dialogue boxes or balloons. While the standard presentation would be not to have much open (white) space in boxes, different lettering styles by artists dictate different approaches to how fill might be used. For instance, in Robert Kirkman and Tony Moore's first volume of *The Walking Dead* (2002, Letterer: Rus Wooton), fill is often also used to suggest tone and enhance a reader's understanding of the storyworld. Thus, when characters whisper the font shrinks in size but dialogue boxes remain large, leaving a larger word balloon with not much written text in it. The size of lettering is just as significant as the size of what contains that lettering. Thus, a critical reader of comics should consider the relationship between captions, balloons, and boxes and the illustrations on a given page. Whether confined by the stark lines or busting free of them, lettering is always spatially oriented on the page: whether through filling a larger container or filling the page space.

Another consideration is panel and page size. Depending on aesthetic styles and illustrators, the rendering of dialogue boxes and sound effects may be uniquely connected to the letterform. Take for instance a moment in Ed Brubaker, Matt Fraction, and David Aja's *Immortal Iron Fist* (2006-2009, letter: Artmonkey Studios), in which the sound effect "BOOM" is used *as* the panel. Here, written text crafted by a letterer is the panel and the art by Aja *fills* the panel. The size of panels is thus dictated by written text and the letterer rather than the reverse case, dictated by the illustrator's design for the page. Similarly, consider the unique transposition of dialogue and panel layout in the first issue of Brian Michael Bendis and Michael Gaydos's *Alias* (2001-2004, letterer: Oscar

Gongora, Richard Starkings, and Cory Petit) in which the placement, size, and alignment of word balloons – joined consecutively over several panels immerses readers in the question-and-answer rapport of private detective and client. Here, position and size, much like the text's easily accessible and *invisible* font, add to the legibility of this scene in the comic.

Typography and Lettering

Although the job of the letterer is to make the comic legible and accessible, in the role that Michael Thomas calls the "back-up singers" to the writers and illustrators' headlining performance, comics creators historically had the option of crafting their own lettering or giving that duty to a typesetter at a publisher. By the 1930s and 1940s the changes in production most often divided the work between an illustrator and lettering artist who would work closely together during the drafting phase.[10] By the 1960s, lettering, as a role, became more distinct, often shifting outside of specific studios or to freelance work in which letterers could work independently of studio and industry demands.[11] In the 1990s, letterers were embroiled in debates between methods of handcraft versus digital creative tools, and it is by this period that the role of the letterer finally began to receive the much missed critical and creative accolades that other components of comic book creating had by 1993 when it became a fully-recognized category in comics' highest honor, the Eisner Award, which started five years previously. Regarding the above historical concerns that are briefly outlined here, critical readers of comic book lettering should consider the overall trends of the industry and the history of comics as a general backdrop for lettering's role in the comic book form. Trends in industry, art, and production deeply impacted lettering – whether these concerns were about creators' rights, technology, or industry standards – and will likely do so in the future.

Regardless of the comic book or graphic novel, it is important to think about both the aesthetic and functional work that the written text achieves, how it does that, and how the letterer successfully creates the writer's script. Whether done by hand or digitally, lettering's unique visual qualities – from font to size to style – can dictate the legibility of comic art. The brief scheme

---

[10] Starkings and Roshell, 6-7.
[11] Starkings and Roshell, 7.

above, as well as the rough outline of lettering's significance in comic book making and comics reading, contextualizes a few primary factors in regards to analyzing and critiquing lettering within comics and serves as a good starting point for a deeper consideration of lettering in future comic reading.

Works Cited

Bechdel, Alison. *Fun Home: A Family Tragicomic*. New York: Mariner Books, 2007.

Chiarello, Mark and Todd Klein. *The DC Comics Guide to Coloring and Lettering*. New York: DC Comics, 2004.

Drucker, Johanna. *The Visible Word: Experimental Typography and Modern Art, 1909-1923*. Chicago: University of Chicago Press, 1993.

Eisner, Will. *Comics and Sequential Art: Principles and Practices from the Legendary Cartoonist*. New York: Norton, 2008.

Kukkonen, Karin. "Navigating Infinite Earths." *The Superhero Reader*. Ed. Charles Hatfield, Jeet Heer, and Kent Worcester. University Press of Mississippi, 2013. 155-169.

McCloud, Scott. *Understanding Comics*. William Morrow Paperbacks, 1994.

Starkings, Richard and Joseph Roshell. *Comic Book Lettering: The ComiCraft Way*. Active Images, 2003.

Thomas, Michael. "The Invisible Art in Plain Sight: A Look at the Art of Lettering." *ComicBookResources* 9 June 2000. Web.

Warde, Beatrice. *The Crystal Goblet: Sixteen Essays on Typography*. Selected, Henry Jacob. Cleveland and New York: The World Publishing Company, 1960.

Further Reading

Bringhurst, Robert. *The Elements of Typographic Style*. 4th Version. Hartley and Marks Publishers, 2013.

Garfield, Simon. *Just My Type: A Book About Fonts*. New York: Gotham Books, 2010.

Gill, Eric. *An Essay on Typography*. 1931. David R. Godine, 2015.

Lupton, Ellen. *Thinking with Type: A Critical Guide for Designers, Writers, Editors, & Students*. 2nd rev ed. Princeton Architectural Press, 2010.

Quick-Draw Creator Interviews

Critics of all backgrounds can learn a lot by listening to the people creating those very works that are subject to review. In our Quick-Draw interviews, professionals from the comics industry share some insights into some of what they feel are the most important about the basic building blocks of comics.

Three Questions on Line Art with Becky Cloonan (*Gotham Academy*, *By Chance or Providence*, *True Lives of the Fabulous Kill Joys*)

Forrest C. Helvie: When looking at a comic, it's clear that the art is what distinguishes a comic from other forms of written narrative. For students or critics new(er) to the medium, what do you think are the most important traits to consider when analyzing the line work (apart from inking and colors) and what about understanding those elements will help readers better understand and appreciate the story being told?

Becky Cloonan: While you read the book, think of this: How does your eye move through each panel? Is the action all flowing in a cohesive direction? Does your eye spill effortlessly from one panel to another? And if not, was the page difficult to read on purpose? Does the panel size and density/decompression evoke or relieve tension? Make a note of how fast or slow you read each page, and then compare that to how the artist has laid the panels out. These are all things I think about when I'm laying out a page; storytelling transcends draftsmanship, technique, or art style. So wether or not you respond to the art in the book is secondary to how well the story is told.

Helvie: Often, readers will refer to the writer as the storyteller. In what ways would you say the line artist also contributes to the telling of the story within a comic?

Cloonan: An artist has to sell you on the story. Their characters have to be designed in a way that reflects their personality, the acting has to be believable. What gestures or facial tics do the characters have? How do characters interact with each other? The chemistry between the characters has to be felt by the reader, the environments need to feel lived-in and real. The artist is bringing this world to life, all this on top of thinking about layouts and pacing. Never cut the artist out of the storyteller equation. Most books I've worked on as an artist I've gotten so much freedom to contribute to the story, and as a writer I always get a ton of story input from artists. I'd go into every book looking at each creative team as an equal partnership. Sure, writers will all have their own unique voice, but paired with different artists that voice can sound very different.

Helvie: Ultimately, how can someone make a determination whether or not the line work in a comic is *good*? Is that even something critics and reviewers should attempt, and if not, what are better ways to approach the work?

Cloonan: Sometimes you have to be able to look beyond your own opinion. For instance, there is probably well-made art, books, movies and music that you for whatever reason just don't like. And other times you'll like something that you know is total garbage (aka the guilty pleasures)! You have to be able to recognize the value in something that you might not personally like, and equally and oppositely true, it's important to be able to enjoy something and be able to critique it at the same time. There are appropriate times to label art as "bad" or "good," but you have to explain why it does or doesn't work, and if that reason is due to personal taste, it's important to recognize that in a critique. Familiarize yourself with the language and syntax of art and comics, and it will boost your appreciation and understanding of the medium!

Three Questions on Inking with Michael Avon Oeming (*Powers, Cave Carson, The United States of Murder Inc.*)

Forrest C. Helvie: As a professional artist with *plenty* of published experience, what's the significance in your mind of inking over the pencils on a page? Why is it necessary from a practical and narrative standpoint?

Michael Avon Oeming: Hmm, I'm not sure that it is anymore. Necessary that is. It is a choice these days, especially with so many artists working digitally. It is faster for more and more artists to "ink" their own pages as they are drawing them. I can't imagine an inker on David Marquez. It would almost be redundant. It all depends on the artist.

Helvie: Does the inker help the writer and artist doing pencils tell the story? How so? (Feel free to address this question from the perspective of having been the only person involved to being a member of a team)

Oeming: Absolutely. Through the use of composition, making lines thicker and thinner, spotting blacks, the inker can help guide the eye to the story points if the penciller fails to draw attention to the subject of the page or panel.

Helvie: Is there anything else you think comic book readers and reviewers don't know when it comes to understanding the significance of the role of the inker but should?

Oeming: It isn't tracing. Even when the pencils are super tight, so tight you can almost shoot from them. It takes years of dedicated practice to lay down perfect lines – and to know when *not* to lay down a perfect line.

Three Questions on Coloring with FCO Plascencia (*Batman, Spawn*)

Forrest C. Helvie: If you had to select one thing that colorists do you think the colorist brings that affects readers the most?

FCO Plascencia: In my personal opinion, I think the most important thing colorist brings is *mood*. I try to bring emotions through color, and that would hopefully help tell the story in a better way.

Helvie: For readers and reviewers who aren't as familiar with the process of coloring, what can you share?

Plascencia: On a more technical side, once I get the drawing pages, (and after staring in awe at the magic Greg and Danny do) my assistants (Sheila, Erika, and Naye) separate the main areas in color on a process called flats. Then I go and choose the color palette based on what I read from Scott Snyder's script or if there is any direction from Greg Capullo.

Helvie: What comes next?

Plascencia: From there I add shade and light in the process called *rendering*. Through coloring, we also make things more "readable." We guide the reader's eyes through focal points, separating planes and differentiating scenes with different color schemes.

Once completed, I get notes from Katie Kubert & Mark Doyle (our editors). When those are completed, the pages are sent to the DC servers from Mexico, where I currently live, and they are ready for Steven Wands to add the lettering.

All that while working hard in order to meet deadlines.

Three Questions on Lettering with Rachel Deering (*Archie Comics*, *In the Dark Vol. 1*, *Anethema*)

Forrest C. Helvie: So I'm curious – as a professional with published experience in lettering, what would you say you bring to the table when you letter a comic?

Rachel Deering: I feel like my biggest contribution to a comic is a well-trained eye for layout and flow. I approach a page in such a way that the placement, size, and shape of my balloons will lead the eye in a very natural way across the page and make the story easier to read. If a reader struggles to understand how to transition from one balloon to the next, you're pulling them out of that story and forcing them to take notice of the lettering itself. As a skilled letterer, it's sort of your job to go unnoticed on first glance, and gain your appreciation on a second or third read through.

Helvie: How can comic readers (and reviewers) identify *professional* quality lettering over more *amateur* quality work?

Deering: The placement of balloons in such a way that the story has a natural flow. Thickness of the stroke around the balloon compliments the lineweight of the inks. Color of the balloon fill and stroke are congruent with or complimentary to the palette of the comic (if the artwork has no stark white and deep black, neither should your balloons, in my opinion). All balloon tails are actually pointing to the speaking character's mouth and not their elbow or asshole. Consistent thickness of the tail where it meets the balloon. An equal amount of breath (the amount of space between the letters and the edge of the balloon) all around the balloon. And my biggest pet peeve: NO TANGENTS!

Helvie: Is there anything else you think comic book readers and reviewers don't know about lettering but should?

Deering: It's not a job that can be expertly handled by just anyone. You can have the greatest writer and the most amazing artist teamed up for a book, but if you slap a shitty lettering job on top, it's like putting diarrhea icing on an otherwise delicious cake. It's a terrible idea. Don't do it!

Navigating Comics

Comics is a medium that is both like and unlike others. When encountering comics for the first time – especially with an analytical lens – it's important to look at the ways in which one might navigate the panels on each page in order to construct meaning from the art and story presented.

How to Navigate Between Panels and Pages: Traditional Reading Protocols in Comics

by Enrique del Rey Cabero

Evidence suggests that comics are finally overcoming past historical prejudices that used to classify the medium as light reading or as exclusively addressed to a young audience. Indeed, comics are becoming increasingly important in our cultural lexicon and are now present not only in general bookstores, libraries, museums and universities but also through multiple reviews in journals, websites and blogs. Partly thanks to the arrival of many adult-oriented graphic novels, comics have increased their public presence both in terms of age and gender through a process which has finally incorporated more women and recovered readers who had stopped reading comics after they grew up. They are increasingly being used as teaching materials in high schools in fields such as history and language learning, in addition to being taken more seriously in academic circles, where they constitute now the object of study in Ph.D.s and university curriculums.

Due to the idiosyncrasy of the medium, comics can be studied from many perspectives and approaches vary enormously. However, there has been a dominant tendency to study them mainly from historical, sociological and thematic points of view, giving importance to content over form, even to the point of completely disregarding this latter element. Among the formal aspects, the reading process and the navigation between the panels and pages are extremely important. As we will see, although it is often taken for granted, it is far from being a simple matter.

Defining comics has proved to be a very difficult task. Every comic is, as Groensteen reminds us, a sophisticated structure that "only actualizes certain potentialities of the medium to the detriment of others" (Groensteen 12). As a consequence, the possibility of establishing a permanent and untouchable definition might be counter-productive and limit the potentialities of the medium. Yet, most people agree in identifying the panel as a basic unit. Panels are arranged in a sequence with other panels (hence the popular name "sequential art" to refer to comics) and separated from each other by panel borders, which help to focus the eye of the reader on a particular space on the page. Panels can have various sizes and be arranged in multiple ways along the page, producing different page layouts (fig. 1). This is one of the defining elements of comics, which are characterised by the cohabitation of images that relate to each other. Although not always the case, most comics make use of rectangular panels with or without a space between them (gutter). The page layout can be regular, using the same size for every panel (fig. 1a), or irregular, making use of different sizes for each panel and/or page (fig. 1b, 1c and 1d). Some regular panel groupings, such as the ones using layouts with six or nine (fig. 1a) identical square panels, have been standardised and been used frequently in the history of the medium. While some authors prefer to alter the size of each panel depending on what they want to depict, thus breaking with monotony, others argue that the repetition of regular layout such as the nine-panel grid actually helps to make the layout invisible and contribute to the reader's immersion in the story.

One of the most important features in comics lies within the relationship between the moments and aspects that the author chooses to represent in the panels and what is not present. The reader, thus, infers what happens in the space of the gutters, an effect which Scott McCloud calls "closure", and "mentally constructs a continuous, unified reality" (67). In this sense, what is left is as important as what is depicted and, together with the size and number of the panels, contribute to create the rhythm of the story. For instance, readers tend to stop and spend more time in larger panels, while a series of smaller panels is frequently read faster and a small panel within another panel (inset) is normally understood as a detail or a secondary action.

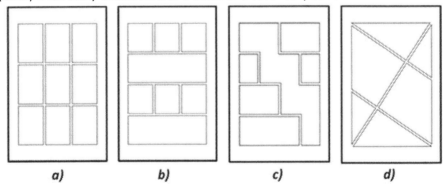

a)   *b)*   *c)*   *d)*

Fig. 1. Some examples of possible page layouts in comics. The possibilities are almost endless, and often different ones are combined in a comic.

Panels are traditionally read from left to right and from the top to the bottom of the page, in a zig-zag path (Z-path) (fig. 2a). This system is inherited from the Western direction of writing and the way the lines end up being read in the codex (book-style format). It is, therefore, a cultural convention. Manga readers are obviously familiar with the fact panels are arranged from right to left and top to bottom in Japanese comics (fig. 2b), following the direction of Japanese script. Therefore, all the elements on the page (speech bubbles, words, sound effects, motion lines, etc.) are also read in this same fashion. This reading order is often preserved in manga translations, usually including some guidelines for readers unfamiliar with this feature. Some publishing houses and authors even refuse to allow their works to be published if they are adapted to the Western left to right reading direction, arguing that it provokes the mirroring of all images. This effect might consequently lead to many differences between the original comic and its adaptation (right-handed characters, for instance, automatically become left-handed).

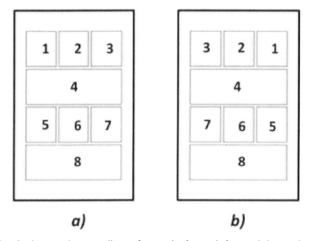

a)   *b)*

Fig. 2. a) shows the reading of panels from left to right typical in most Western comics, while b) shows the reading of panels from right to left distinctive of manga.

Navigating through the panels might look like an easy task in page layouts such as the ones in fig. 1a and 1b. But what about fig. 1c and fig. 1d? The traditional Z-path does not seem to work here, as there is no unique way of approaching the reading of these panels. The cognitive scientist and comic author Neil Cohn has studied in detail, using eye-tracking technology, how readers engage with the panels. He concludes that a reader ultimately approaches comics through "as smooth as reading path as possible" (95-96).

This includes preference of grouped areas over non-grouped areas and smooth paths over broken paths, as well as the inclination not to jump over units and not to leave gaps. This explains the breaking of the Z-path in some panel layouts Cohn provided to his participants (fig. 3b). Natural though it may seem, the Z-path is, as we already mentioned before, a cultural convention inherited from the way we read the lines in a book. Moreover, it might not have been so well established in the early stages of comics. Numbering panels, for instance, was a common practice until the 1930s, probably in order to indicate both the reading order and the fact that the panel was part of a sequence. Windsor McCay, among others, made use of this mechanism in many of his strips (fig. 4).

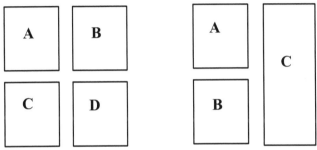

Fig. 3. Two examples of manipulations which Cohn showed to participants in his study: a] grid and b] blockage. Not surprisingly, 94% of the readers followed the Z-path in a], but only 32% did so in b], where they often preferred to first move vertically instead of horizontally [Cohn 94].

It was not uncommon either to place directional arrows to indicate the order in the reading sequence. This was especially relevant when using panel layouts which could potentially confuse readers, such as the one shown in fig. 3b. In this case, if the author would want panel C to be read before panel B, he or she could make use of an arrow between panels A and C and panels C and B, thus guiding the reader's eye. The use of arrows declined once comics become more standardized; however, they are still used in the works of many experimental authors who want to break the linearity of the reading process. Some recent examples include Jason Shiga's *Meanwhile*, a "branching paths"-style comic, and most of the works by Chris Ware. It seems, indeed, that authors are increasingly breaking with the linear approach and engaging with comics in a deeply visual way, and that nowadays even mainstream comics are employing layouts influenced by diagrams and infographics.

Fig. 4. Numbering of the panels can be perceived on the left-hand corner of the panels in this strip of *Little Nemo in Slumberland* from 27 January 1907. It was a common practice at the time.

As a consequence of this experimentation, in some of these works the traditional left to right and top to bottom approach may be broken. The French collective OuBaPo (whose initials roughly translate in English as "Workshop of Potential Comic Art"), among many other experiments, has created comic sequences which can be read in different ways (including reversible and palindrome comics). An increasing number of authors have been experiencing with these and other new possibilities in the last years (fig. 5). Even if these ways of reading comics might seem very original and experimental today, the truth is that many were already present in the early stages of the medium (Gustave Verbeek was already publishing his reversible comics, called *Upside Downs*, as early as in 1903).

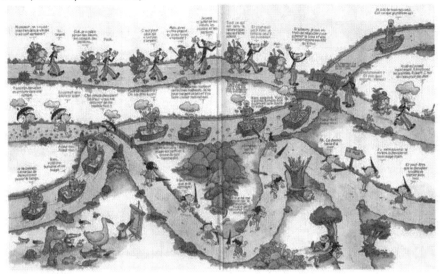

Fig. 5. Sergio García, a Spaniard associated with the OuBaPo movement, has always tried to experiment with the language of comics. The children's comic *Les trois chemins* (*The Three Paths*, 2013), with a script by Lewis Trondheim, makes use of multilinearity, portraying three distinct stories through three reading lines which constantly interact. Drawing itself clearly indicates the reading tracks without the need of panels or further indications.

However, all comics, even more conventional ones, constantly play with two contradictory dimensions: seeing vs. reading. The nature of the page concentrates these tensions, in that it can be read both linearly and holistically. Have you ever ruined your reading of a humorous gag in a comic page by unintentionally looking at the last panel? This is normal: the eye tends to wonder and perceive the whole space of the page, due to what is called peripheral vision. The perception of the images comes first, almost instantaneously; only later a reading path is suggested and the author demands the reader to stop, focus on significative moments (ordinarily, the panels) and – unless it is a silent comic – reinterpret the images in conjunction with the words.

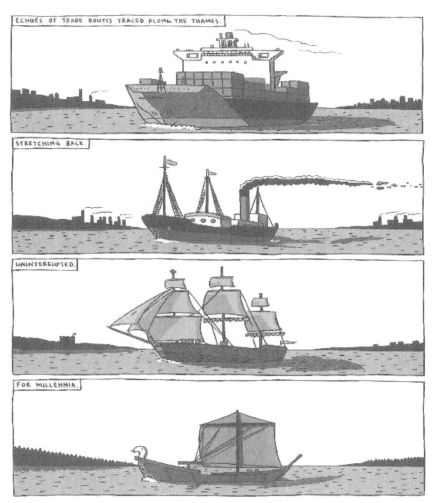

Fig. 6. On this page from Tim Bird's *Grey Area: From the City to the Sea* (2014), a meditation on the passing of time is reflected through the representation of boats from different periods of history. The reader will first acknowledge the structure of the page and the repetition of the motif (identifying common and different elements) before processing each individual panel.

Therefore, panels on the page are "aware" of each other, so authors often conceive pages in an architectural way, establishing a series of correspondences between the images. These include numerous repetitions and variations of aspects such as, just to name a few: color, characters, motifs, orientation of objects and size of the panels (fig. 6). Many artists willing to emphasize the unity of some panels also often transition between them by making use of a continuous background (these panels are also called polyptychs or multi-panels pans). McCay was among the first comic authors to employ this technique, as can be appreciated in panels four, five and six of fig. 4. These three panels, although separated by panel borders, are instantly perceived as a unity thanks to the continuation of the portrayal of the palace and the stairs which the characters are climbing. Yet, they represent different moments in the sequence that the reader also processes linearly. In order to make the drawing more fluid, some authors eliminate gutters, panel borders and even panels themselves, creating a fixed background where characters are represented sequentially just through repetition (fig. 5).

Additionally, it should be noted that, except in the case of comic strips and individual pages (as seen, for instance, in magazines and newspapers), readers most commonly engage with comics through longer formats (such as comic books, albums and graphic novels). Here, except for the first page, a new relevant unit appears: the double-page spread.

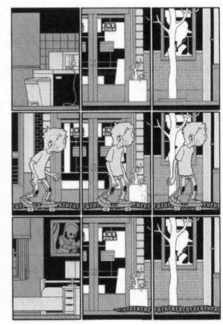

Fig. 7. Antonio Hito's graphic novel *Inercia* (2014) makes a constant use of the double-page spread. In this example, the reader first perceives a clear symmetry in the distribution of colors, which are also coded for spaces (blue being the street or the outside, pink being the house or the inside). We can also observe how the main character wonders around the city on his skateboard through the central panels, which carry on through both pages. There is also some repetition of motifs and the use of continuous background in all the blue panels.

The use of the double-page may vary depending on the author and some prefer to focus on the individual plate. But many conceive it as a pertinent unit (fig. 5, 7, and 8), realizing that the reader is also aware of it when reading a comic and establishing the same kind of correspondences that we saw above in the case of the page. Besides, some artists choose to take into account the passing of pages in their narrative, so they might try to create tension through a cliffhanger in the last panel of a double-page spread in order to resolve it in the next page. This was, for instance, a common technique often used by Hergé in his *Tintin* series.

Finally, it is interesting to observe that the new technologies of digital printing are allowing artists to create comics that break with the traditional book format. Some of these works are also proposing new ways of interacting with the comic-object, such as in the cases of Joe Sacco's *The Great War* (a ten-metre concertina which wordlessly portrays the battle of the Somme) and Chris Ware's celebrated *Building Stories* (a box set containing 14 printed comics in different formats with no determined reading order).

Fig. 8. In *Antatomía de una historieta* [*Anatomy of a Comic*, 2003], Sergio García explores the basics of comics through the medium's form. This double-page spread reflects not only correspondences between the two pages but also a reading direction that breaks with traditional order by making use of the boustrophedon (the reading direction changes every line, repeatedly alternating between left-to-right and right-to-left). The reader can follow this order thanks to the repetition of the main character and the creation of a clear path (which is never interrupted by panel borders or changes of line), such as the ones we saw in fig. 5.

As we have seen, reading a comic is far from being simple and instinctive, but involves a series of complex protocols and processes. Even when dealing with comics that follow a linear approach (left to right and top to bottom) inherited from books, readers are always aware of larger units than the panel, including the page and the double-page spread. The tension between a linear and a holistic reading of comics lies at the heart of the medium's foundation – a tension not easily reproduced in digital comics.

Bibliography

Bird, Tim. *Grey Area – From the City to the Sea*. London: Avery Hill Publishing, 2014.

Cohn, Neil. *The Visual Language of Comics: Introduction to the Structure and Cognition of Sequential Images*. London: Bloomsbury, 2013.

García Sánchez, Sergio. *Anatomía de una historieta*. Madrid: Sins Entido, 2003.

García Sánchez, Sergio & Trondheim, Lewis. *Les trois chemins*. Paris: L'École des Loisirs, 2013.

Groensteen, Thierry. *The system of comics*. Translated by Bart Beaty and Nick Nguyen. Jackson: University Press of Mississippi, 2007.

Hitos, Antonio. *Inercia*. Barcelona: Salamandra Graphics, 2014.

McCay, Windsor. *Little Nemo in Slumberland*. 27 Jan 1907. *The Comic Strip Library*. Web. 15 May 2016 <http://www.comicstriplibrary.org/display/290>

McCloud, Scott. *Understanding Comics. The Invisible Art*. New York: Harper Collins, 1994.

Camera Angles, Panel Framing, and Reader Perspective

by El Anderson

When beginning to analyze or review comics, whether in the context of the classroom or for a news site, it is often the art which we struggle to fully understand. We were taught in school to read a prose novel, break the structure down, and analyze how it tells a story and elicits an impact on the reader. Most of us were not, however, educated in how to do the same thing with the visual side of the art.

Consider this article to be an example of some basic aspects of comic framing, to show you the sort of choices to consider in assessing the composition of a comic. With a basic awareness of what types of creative choices to look for, analysis will be easier, and it will be easier to determine and articulate what it is about a given page that makes it work, or fail.

It helps in beginning to analyze comic art to think of a panel as being 'filmed' by a camera, as we do when we see a still from a movie. Many of the artistic choices in making a comic do not transfer well to film, and vice versa, but this basic idea does.

The 'lens' of the 'camera' determines what we, as the readers, see of the scene. And, as with a movie, there is a person behind that camera making the choices of what we see and how. The simple placement of the 'camera' by the artist can make a tremendous difference to the tone and message of a story. In comics, we describe those choices as 'framing'. Being attentive to framing choices is one of the first skills a reviewer or analyst should master.

Likewise, the artist designs a page with the 'gaze' of the intended audience in mind. This concept is most often raised in terms of the assumed gender (and the accompanying assumption of heterosexuality) of the audience. This is a result of the tendency of a majority of creators in all mediums to assume the audience is male, and to design their art to appeal to the male gaze as a result. It is now increasingly common to see comics intended for a broad audience of all types (the neutral gaze), and the occasional comic drawn with women in mind appear as well. One excellent example of the female gaze is found in the 2014 series *Grayson*, with art by Mikel Janin and Jeremy Cox.

Figure 1. Janin, Mikel, Cox Jeromy; Manguak, Carlos; King, Tom; Seeley, Tim. Nemesis, *Grayson*, DC Comics, 2015.

Grayson struck an excellent balance with powerful women drawn to be attractive and desirable without being overtly sexualized, encouraging the audience to identify with the woman dancing with a man drawn, not to appeal to the ripped masculine ideal common in superhero stories, but to appeal to the female gaze.

The comic industry overall is growing further from the unspoken assumption that they will be read solely by a straight male audience, and this is apparent in the choice to eliminate or reduce the hyper-sexualization of women characters common in the past. While the issue of the assumed gaze of the audience has less overt impact on readers today, as a result of the increasing awareness by artists of their choices, it remains worth considering when assessing a work from an analytical or critical standpoint.

The series *Genius*, written by Marc Bernardin and Adam Freeman, drawn by Afua Richardson, and lettered by Troy Peteri, is an excellent subject for applying these concepts. *Genius* tells the story of Destiny, a young woman who took control of the gangs and residents in a neighborhood to drive away the police, leading to a days-long standoff. Issue 3 opens with Destiny being abruptly surrounded and challenged by the gang members. Her underlings are, effectively, revolting, and in winning them back over, Destiny gives us a master class in how framing and character posture communicates shifting power dynamics.

Figure 2. Richardson, Afua; Peteri, Troy; Bernardin, Marc; Freeman, Adam, *Genius*, p. 6, Image Comics, 2014.

To begin, look closely at the first page and consider the camera placement. We are not viewing this scene from a safe distance, nor are we viewing it from the characters' eye level. We as the viewer are in the circle, hemming Destiny in, alongside the armed men.

Prior to this scene, Destiny was in control and the clear leader of this group, who are now questioning her orders during a violent confrontation with the police. Here, we begin with the camera below eye level, closer to the height of a dog, looking up at Destiny. That angle communicates her power; the group may be confronting her, but they are still subordinates challenging their leader.

You can also see this in the relative height of the characters; every one of these guys is taller than Destiny, but they are positioned and angled in this scene so that even the guy in the red hat is standing with the top of his head ever so slightly lower than the peak of her hair. (Giant feet man is, of course, much taller with the camera at this angle, but his head is off the panel border.) Each man is also aiming *up* at Destiny. Would that work in the real, physics-dependent world? No, they'd likely shoot each other over her head. But here, with the camera in a submissive position, it further adds to her apparent height, making her power apparent, even as her pose communicates the suddenness and threat of the situation. Destiny's feet are spread, but not in a power stance; she appears startled and slightly off-balance. The men, meanwhile, are in classic legs akimbo power poses.

As the challenge continues, Destiny's relative position changes. The challengers appear far more threatening here.

Figure 3. *Genius*, p. 7.

What changed? We are now looking down at Destiny from a spot slightly above her eye level. We are at the eye-level of the men challenging her. The men are mostly taller than her, and the guns are aimed both directly at her head and lower, at her torso. Destiny's hands are up in a somewhat placating gesture, protecting her personal space, and her shoulders are hunched, making her seem smaller and more under siege. Instead of looking up at a leader, we are looking slightly down at another person, as the individuals with the power in this scenario.

Figure 4. Ibid.

But she isn't surrendering. Even as we look down at her from the eyes of the towering gunmen, where Destiny is in a position of submissiveness, she puts on her hood to look bigger and gets that fighting look in her face as she starts to talk.

As she addresses the challengers and answers them, the camera drops back to the level of an equal, meeting Destiny at her eye level as the challengers become listeners and strike passive poses. Already their heads are well below hers again.

Figure 5. Ibid.

Ultimately, the camera drops to a submissive angle, effectively kneeling before her in recognition of her re-established power.

Figure 6. Ibid.

And while the final panel is framed more deceptively, we are basically looking up at destiny from ankle-height and at a respectful distance, communicating that her dominance has been reestablished, and the tension of the argument has diffused. The danger has passed.

Figure 7. Ibid.

Another scene that illustrates the power of framing, particularly when it comes to the evolving depiction of women in comics, comes later in the issue, when a reporter approaches the group in hopes of getting a scoop from the mysterious leader. (She jumped out of a helicopter into a swimming pool to get into the restricted area, hence the wet clothing.)

Throughout *Genius*, the series is mindful of its depiction of women who control and use their own sex appeal. Destiny is attractive, but doesn't dress to the male gaze. (The exception to this is the covers to each issue, but I'll let you reach your own conclusions about marketing departments.) The reporter, meanwhile, is at her most comfortable and relaxed when in business chic. That attire does not serve her interests when approaching this situation, however, so she changes to suit her needs.

Figure 8. *Genius*, p. 13.

Here, we certainly have a powerful, intelligent woman grumbling that she has to dress sexily to get access to the group leader, but that isn't the only message the page sends.

When walking up to the guards, the reporter is shown from a slightly low angle, at a moderate distance away. She is dressed provocatively, but the camera doesn't linger, focus, or dawdle on her attractiveness. This is an example of what I call 'neutral gaze', as the panel is not laid out in a way that is designed to make her look sexy for the reader, even as she sets out to actively appear sexy to the guards.

Then she gets to the guards, and the panel framing shifts unambiguously to the male gaze. The camera

Figure 9. Ibid.

focuses on her butt, at the same level. This angle is more common than you'd think in comics where characters are just chatting, but here it is an intentional choice. As you can see here, this angle tends to lead the characters' eyes to the same focal point we get.

And then the ultimate male gaze panel, where everything from the slightly lowered, submissive head, the tilted body

Figure 10. Ibid.

angle to make her appear smaller, the sultry eyes and the camera angle conspire to achieve her aims of being deemed a non-threat and getting by the guards.

Here, the man Destiny has recruited to pose as the group's leader towers above the two women, in an aggressive stance, but it doesn't work. The reporter changes tactics at once, recognizes the ruse, and is drawn not only at the forefront of the action, but towering over

Figure 11. Ibid.

the other three, the man included. Destiny, meanwhile, is shrinking into the background, with her head at the lowest point, trying to pass as a subordinate.

Figure 12. *Genius*, p. 15.

Note also that, from this point forward, the gaze returns to a gaze closer to neutrality, showing without sexualizing. Even as the reporter gives us a look down her bra, it is incidental to the act of leaning over Destiny in a power-move, and we, like Destiny, understand it as such.

Figure 13. Ibid.

Thus begins a sequence of panels in which the power dynamic slowly switches back from the reporter and her surprise entrance, to women negotiating as equals, and finally back to Destiny, who is in ultimate control of whether the reporter gets what she came for.

Figure 14. *Genius*, p. 17.

And as in the argument scene, the key panel of the encounter is framed from an angle that is low and at a respectful distance, with Destiny relaxed and powerful.

These were just a handful of aspects of *Genius* to consider. There are a million more rules, tricks and techniques that can be identified and assessed, with practice and careful consideration.

In summary, when analyzing a comic, it is important to pause and consider some of the elements discussed above. Identifying the assumed audience of the story based on to whom it is designed to appeal is an important step. The choice of the camera's height relative to the characters communicate volumes of information about who has power and agency in a scene.

Figure 15. Ibid.

Likewise, the panel's angle and the layout of the page also serves to drive both the story itself, and its impact on the reader. As such, these elements merit as much attention and analysis as story and word choice generally receive.

Comics and Cameras: Thinking About Comics Like the Movies

by Jason Kahler (writer) and Stephen Sharar (art)

The visuals of traditional motion pictures have two main purposes: to push forward their narrative and to create emotional resonance. Critics of motion pictures have historically discussed the visuals of motion pictures from those two fronts. Since comic books share many of the same visual techniques of motion pictures, we can read their visuals the same way. Comic book analysts can discuss comic book visuals in two stages, first describing what they observe using motion picture vocabulary, and then unpacking how the visuals contribute to the narrative drive or the emotional impact or the story.

The Whole Picture: Comic Books and Mise-en-Scene

When applied to motion pictures, the term mise-en-scene (from the French meaning "placing on stage") refers to everything the audience sees on the screen. This term was borrowed from critics who wrote about and analyzed stage plays. Mise-en-scene includes physical elements of movies such as set and costume design, props, backgrounds, characters and their positioning, as well as the non-tangible ways which influence how we experience those elements, like lighting. If it's part of what we see on the screen, it's part of the mise-en-scene.

These elements create specific effects on the audience. The elements we observe on the screen can impact our mood, or give us information about the characters or story, for example. In the classic German Expressionist movie *The Cabinet of Dr. Caligari*, the set design – which features odd lighting effects and awkward, angular buildings – contributes to our general feeling of unease and helps us understand the characters' discomfort. Film noir frequently uses low key lighting, with strong contrast between the dark and light areas on the screen. Whatever the effect, a film's mise-en-scene is an important aspect of our relationship with the stories and the characters, and as comic books are similarly a visual medium, we can consider the mise-en-scene of their "screens," as well.

When we analyze a comic book, we can think of its screen as either its individual panels, or consider whole pages at a time. Perhaps an individual panel is noteworthy on its own, for example, a panel with unique or impressive composition, or a panel that has an important reveal. There are certain comics that contain panels that have gone on to be considered iconic: the death of Elektra in *Daredevil* Vol. 1 #181; Green Arrow uncovering Speedy's drug use in *Green Lantern* Vol. 1 #85; any of the final panels from *Batman: The Killing Joke*.

Other times, we might think of the whole page as the screen. When we do this, we still need to consider the contents of the individual panels, but now we also think about how the panels fit together. In a sense, composition of the panels and their respective positions on the page becomes the entire page's mise-en-scene. Consider how the arrangement of the panels influences how our eyes move across the space of the page, how the shapes of the panels might influence our perception of the narrative or the narrative's emotional impact. Perhaps the page makes an interesting use of the white space between panels – called the gutter – or perhaps the panels overlap or interact with each other in a meaningful way.

As we think about mise-en-scene and the connection a comic book has to the movies, it's important to note an important way in which the two mediums are different. Most importantly, comic books (usually) include a text element that motion pictures don't (at least in our modern age of "talkies"). Dialogue balloons, captions, and sound effects make important impacts upon the visual nature of comic books, and though they rarely are meant to represent the physical materials within a comic book's story, they nevertheless become part of our understanding of the visual nature of the book's mise-en-scene.

Many times, the text elements of a comic book are meant to be almost invisible. In these cases, dialogue balloons are the familiar simple ovals with the tails pointing two the speaking character or rectangles that contain the captions. There are times, however, when these text elements break from comic book traditions in meaningful ways. For example, Neil Gaiman's critically-acclaimed *Sandman* series makes interesting use of word balloons: the balloons and the text they contain change as different characters speak. In another example from a DC book, the series *Fables* often featured lavish captions that were as much of the art of the page as the character and background drawings.

Once creators have decided on some of the details of their comic book characters and the characters' worlds, the creators must decide how these details are portrayed. The think about these portrayals, we will turn now to another concept important to filmmaking: the camera and the camera shot.

The "Camera" and "The Shot"

How a comic book creator portrays a scene includes decisions about the pointing of a camera, just like filmmakers, but in the case of comic books, the readers eyes are the camera. Each image is a result of planning and consideration. For example, the opening images of Stanley Kubrick's *The Shining* use elaborate shots thanks to the use of helicopter-mounted cameras. *Touch of Evil*, an important film noir directed by Orson Welles, opens with a long, continuous take with carefully choreographed camera movement and framing. These are examples of shots that last over an extended period, few (or no) breaks. Equally important might be shots that don't last nearly as long. In another Kubrick film, *2001: A Space Odyssey*, the shots of HAL's all-seeing electric eye become disconcerting, and then threatening as the narrative unfolds.

For our discussion of shots and cameras, we'll use two satirical superheroes created especially for this essay: The Point! and his sidekick Hashtag Lad.

The Establishing Shot

An establishing shot is an image that shows the viewer the location in which the story happens. In this way, the shot "establishes" where we are in the story. In these shots, the camera is often zoomed way back, giving the audience a broad view of the scene. So, in the previous example from *The Shining*, the long opening shot serves as an establishing shot, letting us learn that the Overlook Hotel is in a very remote area in the mountains. Comic books employ establish shots in very much the same way, often accompanied with helpful, descriptive captions that give readers even more information about the location.

The image above is a panel showing the not-so-secret hideout for The Point! and Hashtag Lad. This panel works as an establishing shot because it establishes the location of the story and that panels that would follow. From a narrative standpoint, there's not much content, but the emotional content is obviously amusement.

The establishing shot that shows a city is a common device in comic books. Consider, though, the details that might go into such a shot, depending upon the creators' purposes. A bright, clear city, filled with the hustle and bustle of people going about their business feels very different than a shot that features a dark city, filled with shadows and weeping sewer vents, where behind every corner might lurk evil and heartache. In these cases, the mise-en-scene becomes really important because the details generate the intended impact and support the intended story.

Close-ups and Extreme Close-ups

In a close-up shot, the camera is placed or zoomed to give the impression that it's very close to the subject. Often, this is a person's face, but it doesn't have to be. A close-up is a shot that shows the subject in fairly specific detail, yet isn't so close as to completely obscure the background or other context of the shot's composition. A close-up should feel a little intimate without feeling uncomfortable.

The image below is a close-up of Hashtag Lad. A close-up allows the artist to show a lot of detail. The real strength of a close-up is the potential for emotional impact. Here, Hashtag Lad is obviously ready for action, declaring his imminent heroism.

An extreme close-up is a shot that moves even closer to the subject. If the subject is a person, an extreme close-up would be a panel that shows only one aspect of that person, like an eye, for example. In real life, most of us would feel very uncomfortable with a camera that close. Very often, extreme close-up shots feature material items. The murder weapon on the floor, or the face of a clock, perhaps. The acclaimed comic book mini-series *The Watchmen* features a recurring motif of an extreme close-up of a smiley face that reappears over and over throughout the story. Sequences of panels in comic books sometimes begin with extreme close-ups, and then the camera pulls away in subsequent panels to show the subject more fully.

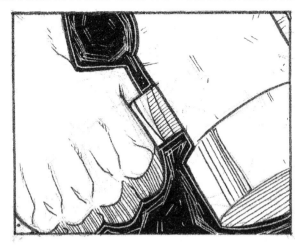

Extreme close-ups can feel very claustrophobic, especially when the subject is a person. Because this shot is employed rarely, it's important to take a note of it and consider its purpose. In the following example of an extreme close-up, the artist wants the reader to almost feel The Point! tighten his grip, ready to fight evil.

Other Shots

A Medium shot would show about half of the shot's subject. If the subject were a person, a Medium shot would show a person from the waist up and fair amount of background detail. A Wide shot would show a person from head to toe, with even more of the background getting drawn into the frame. As the camera pulls away from its subject, detail will be lost. As you can see from the example of the Wide Shot above costumes and props become more important in helping us identify characters as the camera pulls farther and farther away.

We can identify The Point! from his hammer, and Hashtag Lad from his costume. The use of silhouette emphasizes the distance of the Wide Shot.

Narratively, the heroes are making their way through a field. Emotionally, we've returned to the same whimsical feeling that we had earlier with the Establishing Shot.

Angles

We will end our discussion of camera shots with a short consideration of camera angles. In most cases, cameras are placed in fairly neutral angles, level with the subjects' and viewers' eyes, so as to not call attention to the camera's presence. Other times, though, the camera is tilted either up or down to create what we call Low Angle and High Angle shots, respectively.

In a Low Angle shot, the camera is placed toward the bottom of the shot's subject, looking upwards. In comic books as well as motion pictures, Low Angle shots create a feeling of heroism or imposing presence. Throughout comic book history, there  are plenty of examples of the hero making some grand entrance, usually in a splash page, and announcing that he or she is there to save the day. It reminds us that the heroes in comic books are larger than life. The cover of the *Marvels* trade paperback, written by Kurt Busiek and with art by Alex Ross, has a great example of a Low Angle shot via a reflection within a cameraman's lens. In that cover, the sheer size of Hank Pym as Giant Man is emphasized through the upward angle of the Low Angle shot. Here, The Point! and Hashtag Lad look impressive. It's a very different emotional punch than the earlier shots.

High Angle shots employ the reverse: the camera is placed high above the subject and angles downward. The emotional impact of a High Angle shot is the opposite of the Low Angle shot, as well. In a High Angle shot, the subject usually appears vulnerable or small against its background. In our example here, our hearts sink as we understand the odds against which The Point! and Hashtag Lad are facing.

A third angle that warrants mention is what film critics call a Dutch Angle shot. In a Dutch Angle, the camera is usually angled up or down, and also turned on its axis. The effect is very disorienting. Dutch Angles create in viewers extreme feelings of unease, as if the ground isn't quite where it should be, and these shots often imply mania and madness. In modern films, director Sam Raimi often uses Dutch Angles in his *Evil Dead* franchise. In comic books, Dutch Angles can be used in ways that mimic their use in motion pictures, but they can also be used to show a character's movement and abilities. For example, many images of Spider-Man show the character positioned in a traditional way with the page panel, while the background is depicted using a Dutch Angle. This implies that Spider-Man is flinging himself through the scene in every which way and reveals to the reader the exciting nature of his abilities.

Up to this point, we've considered the materials that might be placed into the comic books panels, the mise-en-scene, and the ways in which those materials might be shown, the shot. For the final section of this chapter, we will try to bring to bear one more concept of filmmaking that might seem a little strange at first, considering that comic books are two-dimensional, static words and drawings on a page or screen: camera movement.

Camera Movement

Under the supervision of talented directors and cinematographers, motion picture cameras swing through the air, glide along racetracks, and ride on rafts over plunging waterfalls. The same cameras can wait patiently while subjects of the shot take their time slowly meandering across the screen. Comic book creators don't have the same luxuries when deploying their "cameras," so they rely on framing and the readers' participation in understanding how the images might be "moving." As critics and analysts of comic books, we can apply the vocabulary to help us understand the effects of an artist's camera movement.

A camera is limited to a few basic moves. When understanding how a camera moves through space, it helps to think about our eyes as the camera lens. If we move our gaze straight up or straight down, we are using a "tilt." If we rotate our gaze from left to right, we are "panning." If we move our gaze up or down without tilting, maybe by bending carefully at the knees, that is called a "pedestal." There are other camera movements, and other ways to describe combinations of the movements listed here, but these terms should make it easier to describe what you observe in most comic book stories.

Of course, the pages of a comic book aren't actually moving. Instead, that motion is implied by the changes in the panels shown in sequence. The "movement," then, takes place between the panels, in the gutters, and the reader's imagination understands the motion and fills in the gaps. McCloud calls this mental process of filling in the gaps "closure." Closure is how we understand what happens when we see a character at the top of the stairs in one panel is now at the bottom of the stairs in another. The artist didn't need to draw the character coming down the stairs for us to understand what happened. Closure allows us to experience the motion of the book's camera in the same way that we understand the actions of the character between the page's panels.

Conclusion

As we wrap-up our consideration of comic books and their similarities to the visuals of motion pictures, it's worth noting the potential for tension between critics and fans of both mediums. Film criticism has evolved over the course of over a century, and comic book criticism is still largely in its infancy. We borrow from our film critic colleagues carefully, respectfully, and with appreciation for the language we, too, can employ.

Applying the vocabulary of motion picture critics, describe and then interpret: these are the steps toward a complete visual analysis of nearly any comic book you'll encounter. Through interpretation, consider how the visuals contribute to the narrative, to the emotional impact of the story, or a combination of both.

Works Cited

2001: A Space Odyssey. Metro-Goldwyn-Mayer. 1968.

Batman: The Killing Joke. DC Comics. 1988.

The Cabinet of Dr. Caligari. Decla-Bioscop. 1920.

Daredevil. Marvel Comics. Issue #181, 1964.

Evil Dead franchise. Various distributers. 1981-present.

Fables. DC Comics. 2002-2015.

Green Lantern. DC Comics. Issue #85, 1971.

Marvels. Marvel Comics. 1994.

McCloud, Scott. *Understanding Comics: The Invisible Art*. Harper Collins, 1993, New York.

The Sandman. DC Comics. 1989-1996.

The Shining. Warner Bros., 1980.

Touch of Evil. Universal-International. 1958.

The History and Development of Comics: A Primer

There are complete books and dissertations focused on the history of comics as a medium in addition to the many genres existing within this field of publishing. As such, what we present here serves merely as a field guide of sorts to provide some touchstones for critics who are new to the world of comics. This section will discuss the growth of the medium, some of the genres that have developed within it, as well as some unique characteristics of comics – particularly the superhero genre though not exclusive to it – that critics would do well to consider as they review and critique various comics.

The Elegant Formats of Junk Literature: How Format Shapes the Reading and Interpretation of American Comics Art

by Christopher Haynes

Comics fans face an embarrassment of riches with what and how we read. And yet, in conversations, analyses, and interpretations of comics, publication format often flies under the radar of our attention.[1] Format refers to the materials of comics, the feel of paper and binding, the size and shape of the page, and the platforms and interfaces through which readers encounter them. In some cases, we unknowingly reduce format to a function of genre (e.g. comic books *are* superhero stories). And because our attention is drawn to what's on the page rather than the page itself, it's easy to look right through format. But consciously or unconsciously, the materials of comics shape our reading of them. Recognizing the influence of format on reading practices not only broadens the range of approaches readers can take in their analyses but also unlocks a whole new set of data for consideration. Many different genres inflect the narrative of any given medium, and a single medium finds expression in a broad variety of formats. Attending to these distinctions equips readers to analyze both the narrative and the materials through which they encounter it. Format is the stuff that gives the idea of comics a local habitation and a name.[2]

---

[1] Format in and of itself has received little direct attention by scholars of comics. The standard essay on the subject is Pascal Lefèvre's "The Importance of Being 'Published': A Comparative Study of Different Comics Formats," in *Comics and Culture: Analytical and Theoretical Approaches to Comics*, ed. Anne Magnussen and Hans-Christian Christiansen (Copenhagen: Museum Tusculanum Press, 2000), 91-106. Lefèvre focuses primarily on the ways physical format influences the choices comics creators make.

[2] This essay's title nods to a comment made by Art Spiegelman in an interview from 1980 about RAW magazine: "to have that tension between an elegant format and a medium we're used to thinking of as junk literature makes you look at the work in a different way." Dean Mullaney, "*RAW* Magazine: An Interview with Art Spiegelman and Françoise Mouly," in *Art Spiegelman: Conversations*, ed. Joseph Witek (Jackson: University Press of Mississippi, 2007), 25.

This essay traces comics across their modern history, from newsstands to comic shops, from bookstores to the cloud. Folded sheets of paper, high-gloss or photocopied, bound hardcovers or paperback collections, apps or interfaces: there seems to be no surface able to resist panel and gutter. Format emerges as a focal point for the tensions that mark contemporary comics, tensions between serial and fixed storytelling and between fragmentation of parts and synthesis of wholes. Because of the range of potential material, this essay is selective. It highlights four major format categories: newspaper, pamphlet, book, and digital, presenting examples of each followed by commentary. Consider this essay a point of departure, the start of a conversation that helps readers and writers interrogate not just what's on the page but the experience of the page itself – not just comics stories but the things that make them real, too.

Newspaper

The daily and weekly rhythms of the newspaper business define the modern history of comics. In publication, distribution, and cultural reception, comics and newspapers share cultural space: smeared ink on cheap paper. The characters and gags that populated the papers at the end of the 19th century and the beginning of the 20th set the standard for much of what came after, narratively and structurally. Here is a selective list of newspaper comics' variety of forms.

- **Single panel cartoon:** The single panel cartoon generally contains an image, sometimes driven by a sight gag, sometimes by a moment of powerful affect. It is usually accompanied by a brief caption narrating or describing the scene, as well as limited dialogue.
- **Daily comic strip:** The most easily recognizable of newspaper comics, the daily strip is conventionally black and white, with three or four panels arranged in a row. Daily strips generally contain a standalone joke, but many also build plot and character continuity over time.
- **Sunday comic strip:** Sunday comic strips are bigger (quarter or half page) than daily strips and usually printed in color. As a result of their size, Sunday strips are often more narratively and structurally complex than the dailies. Some daily strips also had Sunday strip versions.

Newspaper strips are defined by their regularity in time. Both daily strips and Sunday strips balance immediacy (the joke) and endurance (many, many jokes across time). There is something comforting about these narrative cycles.

Newspaper strips highlight the investment comics require in time. On some level, we know Lucy will always pull away the football just before Charlie Brown kicks it. But we keep coming back to *Peanuts* just in case. Locating the root of modern comics in the format of the strip, rather than the endearing and heroic characters that eventually grew out of them, highlights how comics follows, and at times shapes, the contours of our daily lives and routines.

Pamphlet

The modern comic book, or "floppy," characterized by folded and stapled paper, is the most visible type of comics pamphlet. The size, shape, and scope of newspaper comic strips is the DNA of this form. One need only stack two to three daily comic strips on top of one another to recognize the standard 3x3 grid of the comics page. But the pamphlet has evolved to be much more than a repository for reprints. Let's look at some examples.

- **Comic book:** Commonly at a size of 10 ⅛" by 6 ⅝", and between 20 and 40 pages (including content, advertisements, and fan letters), the modern comic book is the standard bearer of the medium. Toward the middle of the 20th century, the format evolved from newspaper reprints to original material in a variety of genres, from western and romance to superheroes and science fiction to autobiography and history. Stories in this format are often serialized in monthly or bimonthly installments.

- **Mini-comic:** Mini-comics are generally several inches smaller than comic books (commonly 5 ½" by 4 ¼"), and vary widely in length. Generally self-financed and self-published, mini-comics conspicuously distinguish themselves from corporate publishing. The format is tied to "zine" culture, regularly bought, sold, and traded direct from the creator(s) or at fairs and conventions.

- **Magazine:** Comics magazines are larger in size than standard comic books, and often contain a mix of prose writing and comics content. Magazines often collect and publish material from a variety of creators, sometimes printing excerpts of longer stories.

Short, unbound, and easily distributed: ephemerality defines the pamphlet. In the early 20th century, comic books grew out of the pulps, both in the kinds of stories told and in the quality of the paper used in printing. The materials of the comic book are not built to last. Yet comic book stories extend across weeks, months, years – even lifetimes. Thus, each comic book is both a coherent whole, easily digested with a beginning, middle, and end, and *also* a fragment, part of a story being told across time. Floppies are caught between two conflicting needs: invite the new reader to stay, with dramatic page-turn effects and cliffhangers, *and* reward the devotee with rich internal continuity. Some stories walk this line effectively, others fail at one extreme or the other. Comic book reading is simultaneously brief and recurrent, requiring readers to cycle between short-term immediacy and long-term lineage. Recognizing and communicating this tension is an important tactic when interpreting how comics art makes its meaning.

Book

If strips and pamphlets defined comics through the middle of the 20th century, recent decades witness the rise of the bound book. The evolution from strip to pamphlet to book is fraught with questions of symbolic and material value and acute points of confusion between genre and format. Comics art, in book form, is various: reprints of newspaper strips or short anthologized stories, collections of pamphlets, and fully original material never before published. The following list outlines some of this variety.

- **Trade paperback:** Trade paperback books (TPBs) are generally printed at the same size as comic books, or close to it. Typically, TPBs collect between four and six previously published floppies. TPBs tend to reproduce story arcs and maintain issue sequence. When story arcs exceed the number of issues collected, TPBs are organized by volume number. TPBs usually do not reproduce fan letters or editorial notes, but they do often add variant cover reprints, sketches or other early art, and script pages.

- **Hardcover and Deluxe editions:** Like TPBs, these books collect multiple pamphlets. Varying in size and length, these editions can highlight a particular story arc or an entire series all at once. Often containing supplementary material like TPBs but adding editorial material like introductions and afterwards, these formats enrich the reading experience by adding archival layers.

- **Anthologies:** Another way to compile comics art into books is the anthology (or digest). Hardcover or paperback, large or small, anthologies collect material previously printed in newspapers, comic books, or magazines, and draw together material of varied size, scope, and quality from many different creators. These books are often organized by year, as in the *Best American Comics* series, but also sometimes by creator, style, or subject matter. Due to their multiple nature, anthologies can be difficult to categorize and analyze.

- **Graphic novel:** The graphic novel is difficult to explain. In simple terms, "graphic novel" denotes a single story published as a single book, often branded "OGN" ("original graphic novel"). But the term has been used interchangeably with other bound formats too. Beyond this, the term has been applied ideologically, across formats, to confer legitimacy on the comics medium as a whole via association with a recognizable literary form. Despite its own formal conventions, the graphic novel is an acute instance of the slippage between genre and format: in the bookstore, for instance, you'll find TPBs, deluxe editions, and anthologies of all genres shelved as "Graphic Novels." Reading and writing about graphic novels requires attention to these distinctions. Because there is not yet consensus on what the term "graphic novel" describes, being forthright about the details of each individual book is critical.

In drawing together serial fragments of story into the single instance of the book, bound comics create the perception of coherence. In book form, comics art participates in a long history, both literary and cultural. Comics gains material and metaphorical weight. The book format invites a sustained single engagement with narrative as opposed to one extended periodically through time. Reading a serial floppy (say, six individual stories over six months) is quite different than sitting down to read a trade paperback, telling the same stories all at once. The latter can at times resolve the conflict around the balance of immediate impact and long-term continuity. Changing the reading experience changes the grounds for analysis – we perceive the actions of characters, the recurrence of images and motifs, and the development of themes and concepts on different timescales. As literary readers, we are habituated to identifying patterns as they evolve. Bound comics challenge these patterns depending on the type of aggregation. Recognizing the rich format history of these books is another avenue for analysis and interpretation, no longer defined by the rhythms of the newspaper or the economics of pamphlet publication.

Digital

If bound comics disrupt the rhythms of the strip and the pamphlet, digital comics challenge the idea that the form is limited by space and time in the first place. Comics stories told digitally might be as simple as a scanned PDF or as complex as a device interface responding to multi-touch gestures in real time. While digital comics often retain the formal conventions of panels, grids, speech balloons, and thought bubbles, they reframe the relationship these elements create with readers, pushing boundaries of interactivity. Let's explore a few examples.

- **Digital comic:** Digital comics range from digitized print material to stories created, published, and consumed in digital environments. Generally available through online platforms for purchase in .pdf and .cbr file formats, digital comics can be archived in the cloud, downloaded directly, or read right in a web browser. Digital comics often deviate from standard page counts and story lengths, riffing on the standard shape and scope of the comic floppy. Often, readers can choose to move linearly page to page, or interactively panel to panel. Some digital comics platforms offer a "guided view," which takes readers panel-by-panel, and sometimes detail by detail, with each tap or swipe, simulating the anticipated movement of the eye down the page.

- **eBooks:** Some longer comics stories are published as eBooks in .pdf and .epub file formats. eBooks might be static pages, readable on most e-reading devices (like Kindle and Nook), or they might be interactive, engaging the device interface to manipulate how readers move through the story through touches and gestures. In some cases, the electronic version of a comic introduces interactive features not possible in the print iteration of the same story.

- **Webcomics:** Webcomics are difficult to categorize precisely because they take many forms and replicate many formats. While some webcomics are strips or stories published serially online, some are fully immersive narrative environments requiring a high degree of interaction through page navigation, scrolling, clicking, and hyperlinking. Some are hosted on blog platforms, some have their own dedicated domains. Because there are no material limitations, many webcomics play with dimension, scale, user experience, and different reading modalities. Most webcomics are accessible for free, but some provide premium access or features with subscription fees or donations.

With digital comics, the operative word is interface. The reader may click through pages, swipe between panels, zoom in and out of image or text elements, or hit play and be guided by the interface itself. Digital comics have a greater potential for interaction – print comics can be interactive as well, but digital comics and webcomics have their own native strategies for narrative immersion. The affordances of the digital format reshape the relationship between comics and readers in space and time, and call attention to the influence format exerts on that relationship. Comics have always been a participatory medium, but digital comics and webcomics heighten the role participation plays in the construction of narrative experience from the start. They invite us to consider the experience of reading and the analysis of narrative together. In fact, they suggest that the two are inseparable.

Conclusion

As much as I have tried to categorize it, comics art never respects the boundaries of a list. It infiltrates and adapts, assimilating and at times guiding the changing conditions of publishing, distribution, and consumption. Take, for example, a canonical comic like Art Spiegelman's *Maus.* Beginning its life as a short story in an anthology (1972's *Funny Aminals*), *Maus* evolved into a series of pamphlet inserts in *RAW* magazine (starting with Vol. 1 No. 2 in 1980) and individual chapters in *RAW*'s digest TPBs (starting with Vol. 2 No. 1 in 1989). Two separate TPBs collect these serialized fragments: *Maus: A Survivor's Tale Vol. I: My Father Bleeds History* (1986) and *Maus: A Survivor's Tale Vol. II: And Here My Troubles Began* (1992). And these TPBs have been collected into *The Complete Maus* (1996) and *MetaMaus: A Look Inside a Modern Classic* (2011). *MetaMaus* includes a digital edition of *Maus* and archival material on DVD. *Maus*, it is clear, has never been confined to a single format, and each instance of the story frames the reader's experience of it in unique ways.

No matter how elegant the scheme, comics will always find a way to escape. Therefore, I want to close with three guiding principles for attending to format as you read and analyze comics art. First, format differences create and sustain particular relationships between reader and story. Degradable newsprint and acid-free pages bound in a hardcover book feel very different in your hands, and therefore *mean* different things to you as you read. Second, format is not passive. It asserts itself by drawing a reader's attention to the experience of reading itself. This presence is strategic, influencing analysis and interpretation. When writing about comics, account for format's active presence. Finally, and this is the most important point: follow the invitations of format, but be aware that while those invitations pull you toward certain narrative or formal elements, they may also pull you away from others. The best strategy is to think critically about the page, as well as what's printed on it, in equal measure.

Bibliography

Pascal Lefèvre, "The Importance of Being 'Published': A Comparative Study of Different Comics Formats," in *Comics and Culture: Analytical and Theoretical Approaches to Comics*, ed. Anne Magnussen and Hans-Christian Christiansen (Copenhagen: Museum Tusculanum Press, 2000), 91-106.

Dean Mullaney, "*RAW* Magazine: An Interview with Art Spiegelman and Françoise Mouly," in *Art Spiegelman: Conversations*, ed. Joseph Witek (Jackson: University Press of Mississippi, 2007), 20-35.

Is a Comic Book a Book? Considering the Materiality of Comics

by Laura R. Braunstein

How and why should we regard the comic book as a book? *Should* we regard the comic book as a book? That is, how do considerations of comics as material culture add to, enhance, and complicate our understanding and analysis of comics as narrative and as art? For much of its history, the comic's status as an ephemeral object – something printed on low-quality paper, bought by adolescents from a revolving wire rack at a drugstore – has forestalled its consideration as art and literature. Given this history, what should writers and critics look for when considering the materiality of the comics that they analyze, review, and recommend? This chapter will give a brief overview of the material culture of comics, while providing readers with a series of discussion points on how attending to the material aspects of the comic book *as a book* enhances scholarship and criticism.

Longtime comics librarian Randall Scott may have startled some when he stated that "It is normal to treat rare books with respect for the physical item, but it is a rare reader or librarian who will automatically treat a comic book with the same respect. The average plain old comic book is probably more fragile than the average Gutenberg Bible, after all."[3] Why is this? Before the 1980s, most comics, like newspapers, were printed on wood-pulp paper. Wood-pulp paper began to replace cotton and linen rag paper in the mid-nineteenth century, around the time of the rise of mechanized printing – an industrial development that also led to the development of the mass-market "dime novel" and one of its successors, the comic book. Both the production processes for wood-pulp paper and the chemicals used in its manufacture contribute to its potential for acidification. That is, the very materials inherent in the physical composition of many comic books ensure their eventual

---

[3] Randall Scott, *Comics Librarianship: A Handbook* (Jefferson, NC: McFarland), p. 46.

deterioration (book conservators call this "inherent vice").[4] Collectors and librarians have many strategies to combat the deterioration of comic book paper, from using mylar envelopes to keeping collections out of direct light to restricting the use of original copies. Understanding book history in regard to comics is important for comics scholars, critics, and students alike. Comics writers often focus primarily on *content*; knowing the contexts in which comics appear as *form* – how comics are books – can better prepare writers to critique story, characters, and art.

The field that studies books as physical objects is called *descriptive bibliography*. While most students of comics are not rare-books historians and should not be expected to be trained in descriptive bibliography, it can help to understand a few of the questions that bibliographers ask when they consider a book as an object. The first question is: what is this object that you are going to write about? Or, put another way, what is the printed[5] container in which the comic narrative appears? What most people imagine when they picture a comic book is the item that collectors call a "floppy": one issue of a series (say, *Uncanny X-Men* #129), published periodically, and consisting of stacked or nested sheets stapled together in what is known as a *saddle-stitch* binding. Most mainstream series are still published this way, as are many small-press and self-published comics. Floppies are generally displayed in comic book shops in front-facing racks, or in the magazine sections of bookstores, and rarely found with their spines facing outwards on bookstore or library shelves. Some libraries will collect and bind multiple issues or a run of, say, a year, much like they bind annual volumes of magazines and journals. In response to this practice, there are distributors that now specialize in durable library editions of comics, specifically produced to withstand the rigors of circulation.

When periodical comics originally issued serially are collected and republished (by publishers, as distinct from being rebound by libraries), they appear in *trade* editions. Trade editions have higher-quality paper, a thicker,

---

[4] Library of Congress, *The Deterioration and Preservation of Paper: Some Essential Facts*, 2002. www.loc.gov/preservation/care/deterioratebrochure.html Retrieved June 5, 2016.

[5] This discussion focuses on the comic as printed medium; webcomics, with their potential for what Scott McCloud has called the "infinite canvas," demand another set of criteria. See McCloud, *Reinventing Comics: How Imagination and Technology are Revolutionizing an Art Form* (New York: Perennial, 2000).

glossier cover, and a glued or sewn squared-off spine, also called *perfect binding*. Graphic novels and other single-issue, long-form (namely, not issued serially) comics are also published this way. When large general-interest media companies (such as Pantheon Books) publish original graphic novels (i.e. those that have not already been serialized as floppies), they tend to be issued first as cloth-bound hardcovers, and then as trade paperbacks, much like new fiction. Original graphic novels, in their design and marketing, signal their prestige in the media industry by employing the aesthetics of literature; they look like books that you would buy in a bookstore. Trade editions of series often emulate original graphic novels in physical attributes such as size, shape, and paper quality, as well as in the attention given to cover images and other design elements. If the original graphic novel is the publishers' prestige item, meant to position the comic as a cultural intervention into the arena of literature, then the trade collection has a similar presence, as if to tell the reader, look: this has been transformed from entertainment to art.

Some comics publishers continue to reprint individual series titles in different formats. Neil Gaiman's groundbreaking *Sandman*, for instance, is available from DC Comics as a series of trade volumes with the same *trim size* (or paper dimensions) as the original comics, a two-volume "Omnibus" edition with larger recolored pages, and an oversized "Absolute" edition in a slipcase – all of which have different ancillary material.[6] While some may cynically call this a scheme to capitalize on a title's popularity, having a variety of editions can attract new readers and expand the reach of writers and artists. As well, publishing or republishing comics as books is one way to establish that the comic is worthy of literary and artistic regard, and not just disposable entertainment. Comics scholar Dale Jacobs suggests that the rise of the graphic novel in the 1980s as a medium independent of serially issued floppies led to the incorporation of comics into library collections, and thus was one step in legitimizing comics as a form of art and literature: "because the graphic novel looked like a physical book and often included subject matter that was not aimed strictly at children, librarians were able to conceptualize it *as a book* and thus worth of a place in their collections."[7] Note that while Jacobs's point is well

---

[6] I am grateful to Scott Nybakken for enumerating these details.

[7] Dale Jacobs, *Graphic Encounters: Comics and the Sponsorship of Multimodal Literacy* (New York: Bloomsbury, 2013), p. 206. Emphasis in original.

taken, he erroneously conflates the graphic novel as interchangeable with the comic book as a medium, whereas it is actually one format employed within the medium.

Thinking about the comic as a material object, then, can help students and critics understand how a particular comic is meant as a cultural intervention. Is it a single issue in a series, available for a few dollars? Or is it a complete narrative contained in one package, at a higher price? Does the cover reprint art from a serial issue, or has it been redesigned or embellished? Is it meant to be shelved with other items in a collection, or displayed as an art object, like a coffee-table book? These are clues to the intended prestige of the comic: artists, writers, editors, and publishers all contribute to a decision about whether we are meant to see it as entertainment or as art. (Or both.) How are readers intended to engage with the comic as an object?

Thinking about the comic as a book or an object should not be separate from thinking about the comic as a story told through sequential art. Many creators incorporate considerations of the materiality of their comics into art and narrative. As comics scholar Charles Hatfield argues, comics use form to "communicate or underscore" content: "many comics make it impossible to distinguish between text per se and secondary aspects such as design and the physical package, because they continually invoke said aspects to influence the reader's participation in meaning-making."[8] Hatfield's argument takes our original question – is a comic book a book? – and extends and complicates it. If the comic book is a book, how does it, as a book, make demands on its readers in order to produce meaning? Or, put another way, how does the comic use its materiality to invoke the reader's response? As an example, consider Art Spiegelman's *In the Shadow of No Towers*.[9] Spiegelman refracts his family's experience during the September 11, 2001, attacks on New York City through his connoisseurship of vintage newspaper comics. The book's oversized, rectangular shape suggests both the tabloid page size of old papers and the looming towers of the World Trade Center. Writing about *In the Shadow of No Towers*, comics scholar Katalin Orbán notes that the book's "sense of materiality is thus established primarily through a tactile relationship, in which

---

[8] Charles Hatfield, "An Art of Tensions," 132-48 in Heer and Worcester, eds., *A Comics Studies Reader* (Jackson, MS: University Press of Mississippi, 2009), p. 144.
[9] Art Spiegelman, *In the Shadow of No Towers* (New York: Pantheon, 2004).

hand-book contact and haptic visuality mutually inform each other."[10] The term *haptics*, from the Greek *haptós* or "touch," is concerned not only with visual and tactile perception, but with the interaction of the perceiving subject (say, the reader) with an object (say, the comic) through space and time. The oversized shape of *In the Shadow of No Towers* prompts its readers to consider their relationships in space to the objects they're holding. Thinking of comics as material culture, then, is an exercise in the haptics of art and reading.

In his classic, groundbreaking book *Understanding Comics*, Scott McCloud frames one role of the reader of sequential art as creating closure across panels.[11] The reader's engagement invests the art, story, and design of the comics narrative with meaning by connecting sequences of panels to each other over time. While McCloud refers only to the reader's presence within the content of a comic story, we can extend his discussion to a consideration of the entire book. If comic books are books, how are they books? How do they demand or evoke a certain interactive experience from the reader? In writing about comics, we – as students, scholars, and critics – recreate and explicate this experience in turn for our readers. We owe it to them to fully engage with the visual, narrative, and haptic registers of the comic books we read.

---

[10] Katalin Orbán, "A Language of Scratches and Stitches: The Graphic Novel Between Hyperreading and Print," *Critical Inquiry* (Spring 2014) 40.3: 173.
[11] See Scott McCloud, *Understanding Comics: The Invisible Art* (Northampton, MA: Kitchen Sink Press, 1993), particularly Chapter 3: "Blood in the Gutter."

Comic Genres: An Historical Overview

by Philip Smith

This chapter seeks to provide a brief historical survey of the various genres of comics, offering a taxonomy, history and stylistic "spotter's guide" for the major broad categories of comics. Such a study is, of course, fraught with challenges. Distinguishing where one genre ends and another begins is often a highly subjective and contested activity. Boundary-markers such as time period, business model, affiliation, degree of formal experimentation, or subject are not entirely reliable determiners of genre. As shall be evident in the discussion that follows, it is better not to think of comics genres as discrete, but permeable and ever-evolving. Comics, like all media, are an ecosystem, where changes in one genre inform and give rise to others. I have chosen to present genres in a historical format because this will allow me to illustrate the ways in which given genres have changed over time.

Space limitations mean that no survey can fully encompass every genre of comics (if such a feat even could be attempted). This chapter will, therefore, focus on the major genre classifiers found in American comics, namely the editorial cartoon, three-panel "gag," horror, romance, detective, non-fiction, underground, art, erotica, alternative, superhero, and funny animal comic. Other genres, most notably those found in manga, regrettably, remains beyond the purview of this work.

Early Comics

Characteristics: Use of woodcuts; Captions; Single images

Comics have roots in the earliest printed works in Europe which combined images and text. John Foxe's *Book of Martyrs* (1563) and John Bunyan's *Divine Emblems* (1686) are examples of this kind of work. Many scholars trace the origins of modern comics to the nineteenth century where Rodolphe Töpffer (1799-1846), Gustave Doré (1832-1883), and the Forrester brothers using the pseudonym "Alfred Crowquill" (1803 / 1804 to 1872) worked with woodcuts (some scholars claim art such as the Bayeux Tapestry as even earlier precursors of modern comics, but it is unlikely you will be asked to review such works, so I have not addressed them here). Töpffer produced several works which combined words and pictures as well as writing essays on the form. "Crowquill" wrote and drew for the British humour magazine *Punch* (1841-2002).

Editorial Cartoons

Characteristics: Short (often one panel); Speech often appears in a caption rather than a speech bubble; Humour; Often engages with a topical news item; Appears in newspapers or collected anthologies

During the 19th century, English magazines, perhaps most famously *Punch*, used captioned drawings, called cartoons (or "editorial cartoons") for humour and social or political commentary. A cartoon typically features a single image with a caption, often embedded within or alongside a newspaper page. Typically the caption delivers the "punch" of the humor. Cartoons often seek to offer a humorous comment on a contemporary news item. This genre of comics continues to thrive in newspapers and magazines today. During the nineteenth and early 20th-century European-style cartoons began to appear throughout the world, helped by the spread of European imperialism. The first generation of comic book creators in America, such as Richard F. Outcault, who drew *The Yellow Kid* (1895-1898), continued to use the single-image editorial cartoon format.

Three Panel "Gag" and "Sunday Funnies"

Characteristics: Typically a joke told in three panels or half-page; Recurring characters; Humour; Appears in newspapers or collected anthologies

During the early 20th century, America also saw a dramatic increase in newspaper comics, both short "gag" comics and "Sunday Funnies" – multi-panel single or half page comics which appeared in the Sunday editions of various newspapers. Three-panel "gag" cartoons, which have now become the standard format for newspaper comics, typically feature recurring characters and a three-panel format with the final panel delivering a punchline. Some have ongoing storylines. Sunday funnies are often a longer form version of shorter "gag" comics and feature the same characters, although some stand alone. Even within the Sunday funny genre there is considerable thematic and visual variation. Windsor McCay (1869-1934), for example, drew surreal and beautiful images in *Little Nemo in Sulmberland* (1905-1914 and 1924-1926), whereas Frederick Burr Opper (1857-1937) created humorous and slapstick comics such as *Happy Hooligan* (1900-1932).

Funny Animal

Characteristics: Anthropomorphic animal characters; Aimed at children

"Funny animal" comics – featuring animal characters who walk on two legs, have jobs, and otherwise act like humans – began to appear at the same time as "Sunday Funnies," creating a genre of comics aimed primarily at children. The leading exemplar of this genre was, and continues to be, comics featuring Disney characters.

Crime

Characteristics: Longer format than earlier comics; "Noir" genre markers such as the hard-drinking detective, the "femme fatale," city setting, heavy use of shadow, etc.

In the 1920s, longer-form comics such as *Comics Monthly* (1922) and *Comic Cuts* (1934) began appearing in a larger format as standalone publications. Many of these titles compiled or offered multi-page versions of existing humor comics. This longer form of comics allowed creators to offer storylines with greater narrative complexity than the simple jokes which had graced the pages of newspapers previously. The early 20th century was an explosive period in comics publishing where new titles appeared with rapid frequency and were consumed in large numbers. Several genres emerged during this time such as the detective (or "crime") comic (most famously Chester Gould's *Dick Tracy* (1931-present)), which embodied elements of the "noir" genre of film such as chiaroscuro (heavy use of light and shade) lighting, voice-over narration, and themes of crime. The genre enjoyed its heyday in the 1930s and 1940s, and fell victim to the anti-comic crusade of the 1950s. It survives, however, in Ed Brubacker and Sean Philips *Criminal* (2007-present)*,* as well Frank Miller's *Sin City* (1991-2000). These modern crime comics contain many of the characteristics as earlier incarnations of the genre, along with more explicit violence and what we might call a postmodern self-awareness.

Golden Age Superhero

Characteristics; Superhero protagonist (costumed character with super-powers); World War II; Crime-fighting theme; Somewhat simplistic characters compared to later iterations of the genre

The superhero genre appeared for the first time in the late 1930s and reached its heyday during World War II. Early "Golden Age" superhero comics such as *Action Comics* (1938 – 2011), which gave the world Superman, featured protagonists with extraordinary powers but borrowed thematically from the detective genre in that they generally revolved around crime-fighting. The superhero comic was singularly suited to propaganda purposes, and many early superheroes were depicted fighting on the side of the Allies as part of World War II (although more often on the cover than in the pages). Typically the morality of these comics was somewhat stark, dividing humanity into those who are impossibly good and those who are irredeemably evil. These comics proved hugely popular with American servicemen, leading to their dissemination in Europe and Asia where they influenced local creators. The superhero genre, as we shall see, later, has transformed considerably since these early days.

Horror

Characteristics: Werewolves, vampires, and other otherworldly creatures; Mad scientists; Extreme violence; Psychological horror

The crime genre also gave rise to horror comics such as *Adventures in the Unknown* (1948-1967), which featured monsters and, often, grotesque imagery. Some horror comics made reference to world events such as the Holocaust or the anxiety over nuclear arms buildup during the (then ongoing) Cold War. Many individuals considered these violent comics to be obscene and completely unsuitable for children. The horror genre often informed, and was informed by crime, romance, superhero, and detective comics, with, for example, horror elements creeping into superhero comics. The genre enjoyed a brief revival in the 1970s and is sometimes referenced in modern comics such as *The Sandman* (1989-1996) or *The Goon* (1999-present).

Romance

Characteristics: Relationships; First-person narration (in voice-over panels); Young female protagonists.

The early 20th century also saw the emergence of romance comics such as *Young Love* (1947-1977) – soap opera-style comics marketed primarily at housewives. The genre was characterized by themes of relationships, divorce and heartbreak, first-person narration, and female protagonists in their late teens and early 20s. This genre has now largely vanished (surviving in the long-running *Archie* series and Roy Lichtenstein paintings), but once occupied a large share of the comics market.

Silver-Age Superhero

Characteristics; superhero protagonist (costumed character with superpowers); Crime-fighting theme; Emotionally-flawed superheroes with problems that more-closely approximate those of their readers, iconic identity (including costume), and superhuman powers or uncanny abilities.

During the 1950s comics came under attack. A series of books and articles criticized comics for causing juvenile delinquency and retarding the development of literacy. In response, comic book creators began self-policing through the Comics Code Authority (CCA), which set stringent guidelines on comics content. Many comics retailers refused to carry comics which did not carry the CCA stamp. This led to a decline in the crime, horror, and romance genres. The late 1950s and early 1960s was the "Silver Age" of superhero comics. The Silver Age is characterized by artistic and storytelling temperament of Jack Kirby and Stan Lee, with a generation of superheroes who were flawed and self-doubting. Silver Age comics often concern moral crises and more complex moral questions than those of the Golden Age.

Underground

Characteristics: Drug use; Violence; Autobiography; Politics; Social commentary; Experimentation; Independent publication

The CCA also gave rise, unintentionally, to underground comic (or "comix"). Underground comics are creator-owned publications written (broadly) during the 1960s and early 1970s. Perhaps the most famous among those working in the genre are Robert Crumb (1943-present) and Art Spiegelman (1948-present). The creators of these comics sold their works by hand or through "head shops." These comics engaged with subjects such as "free love," drug use and politics, as well as offering an extravagant foregrounding of comic book form. The stylistics of this genre varied considerably, but consistently erred away from the chiseled features found in many superhero, romance, and detective comics. The primary genre of the underground was autobiography. As with other genres, the underground comic did not develop in isolation; the humor magazine *MAD Magazine* (1952-present), *Puck* (1871-1918) and the pornographic parody Tijuana Bibles (1920s onward) all, in different ways, preceded and inspired work in the underground comic scene. Underground comics undoubtedly changed the comic book medium (particularly in terms of business models and creator-centric works), but the genre can be viewed as a continuation of pre-CCA themes rather than as a complete departure from everything which had come before. The underground can be divided loosely into two waves: the first wave focused upon taboo subjects and shocking images as a reaction against the self-imposed censorship of other comic book genres. The second wave during the early 1970s saw a surge of comics which explored social issues such as feminism, sexuality and politics.

Alternative

Characteristics: Experimentation; Autobiography; Political and emotional sophistication; "Adult" subjects such as sex, approached in a mature manner

From the mid-1970s onward the "alternative" or "independent" comics genre emerged which continue the underground's legacy of formal experimentation, hypertextuality, psychological realism and a willingness to approach subjects which, during the height of the Comic Code Authority, had been considered beyond the remit of the form. This was the result of the publication of three high-profile comics – *Maus Vol. I* (1986), *The Dark Knight Returns* (1986), and *Watchmen* (1987) – which demonstrated a level of political and emotional sophistication. In the wake of this event, many comics appeared which avoided the characteristics of what we might term "mainstream" comics in terms of story and aesthetics, preferring, instead, exploration of taboo subjects and characters who are caught in "adult" dilemmas. Unlike underground comics, many alternative comics were produced by large publishing companies and some featured unironic appearances from well-established characters from other comic book genres. The success of lines such as DC's Vertigo imprint suggests that the term "independent" is not wholly accurate. "Alternative" is now the broadest category of comics, not least because those working in the genre are characterized by a stylistic commitment to innovation. An alternative comic, almost by definition, seeks to be different from every other alternative comic. During the 1990s the alternative genre included works from DC's Vertigo line such as Neil Gaiman's *The Sandman* (1989-1996) and the experimental work which appeared in Art Spiegelman and Françoise Mouly's magazine *RAW* (1980-1991). Modern alternative comics include those by Chris Ware (1969-present), Marjane Satrapi (1969-present), and Sonny Liew (1974-present).

"Alternative" has become something of a misnomer, as the genre has influenced almost all comics produced during the late 20th and early 21st centuries. The alternative genre arose concurrently with the grittier "modern age" of superhero comics, which includes a greater emphasis on social issues and real-world politics. Some superhero comics have also embraced the commitment to stylistic experimentation of the alternative genre, including, for example, the formal experimentation found in Matt Fraction's *Hawkeye* (2012-2015).

"Art" Comics

Characteristics: Highly experimental approach; Abstract themes; Prioritisation of stylistics over story

Within the "alternative" genre we might further distinguish highly experimental "art" comics which, following the legacy of *RAW*, focus on testing and expanding the comic book form. Examples of "art" comics would include Aidan Koch's *Blue Period* (which appears in *Best American Comics 2014*), or Julie Morstad's *The Wayside* (2012). These comics often prioritise art over story, and take a surrealist approach to their subject. They are often characterised by play with color shape, flow, and time.

Erotic Comics

Characteristics: Sex themes; Written primarily for titillation; Some humour

The growth of "Sunday funnies" led to the development of pornographic parodies called "Tijuana bibles," featuring recognizable characters in sexual scenarios. The underground genre, in part, took its cue from Tijuana bibles in its graphic depictions of sex. The underground tended to use sexual content for shock or humour rather than titillation, however. Nonetheless, erotic comics (sometimes called "pornographic" or "sex" comics) owe much of their development to the "anything goes" taboo-breaking spirit of the underground. This genre, as one might guess from the title, centers upon sex acts and, often, humour. Erotic comics include titles such as *Black Kiss* (1988) and *Leather and Lace* (1989). Erotic comics have truly found their home with the development of the internet, where numerous sites such as *8muses.com* offer free or paid-for erotic content.

Non-Fiction

Characteristics: Instructional content; Detailed images

Another genre to arise during the latter half of the 20th century is the "non-fiction" or "essay" comic. Comics have proven to be a practical means to convey technical information including, for example, manuals for the M16 assault rifle issued to American soldiers in Vietnam. As a result of the rise of alternative comics, long-form versions the non-fiction genre have also emerged, perhaps most famously those by Scott McCloud in his series of books beginning with *Understanding Comics* (1992). We might also include in this genre titles such as *The Cartoon Introduction to Philosophy* (2015) which takes a light-hearted narrative tone, biography such as *Logicomix* (2010), or the depiction of historical events such as *March* (2015 and 2016).

Adaptation / Translation

Characteristics: Retells a story from another medium; Often has an educational purpose

The accessibility and popularity of comics as a medium has meant that several comic book creators have adapted other media to the comic book form. Most popular among these media are works of literature and plays. Given Shakespeare's standing in both popular culture and on English Literature courses, it is perhaps unsurprising that comic book Shakespeare adaptations have been available since the 1950s. The multi-volume *Graphic Canon* (2012-2013) is perhaps the most well-known work in this genre. The first volume contains comic book renditions of literary works from ancient times to 1700 including Gilgamesh and Shakespeare's plays, the second volume concerns the nineteenth century, including fairy stories and Romantic poetry, and the third volume covers the 20th century, ranging from *Heart of Darkness* to *Infinite Jest*. These works are generally implicitly educational – in many cases they are designed as a more accessible alternative to purely textual works. They also represent an interpretation, or version of a given story which may contrast with other readings of a given text.

Webcomics

Characteristics: Published online; Can be any genre

The rise of the internet has expanded the reach of all comics genres – the three panel gag format has become the standard for webcomics as it is for newspapers. The web has also given rise to the possibility of far more experimental comics including additions such as animation and the "infinite canvass" of a web page.

Classifying a particular comic is often a challenge. What are we to make, for example, of Brandon Graham's *Multiple Warheads* (2003 and 2013), which began life as a sex comic but grew into an alternative comic with occasional erotic moments, or Neil Gaiman's *The Sandman* – a mythical story which, at times occupies the horror, superhero, and "art" genres and yet seems to transcend them all, or Art Spiegelman's *Ace Hole: Midget Detective* (1974), an experimental detective parody published at the height of the underground era. As with any taxonomy, defining comics by genre often raises as many problems as it solves. Rather than seeking to locate a particular title within its network of influences, then, it is perhaps important simply to acknowledge that comics come in many forms and even the most seemingly generic of superhero comics represents only one moment in an ever-evolving and ever-expanding medium.

Continuity and Deep Fictional Universes: Superhero Comics and Historical Criticism

by Jeffrey Hayes

One of the joys of engaging with superhero comics is the way I as a reader am able to have a personal experience with a larger shared fictional universe. But how deep are these fictional universes? How far back do they go? In the vein of classic "choose your own adventure" books, the universes of DC and Marvel offer many choices for reader experience. That choice, however, is different in that a "choose your own adventure" story is about constructing a narrative, while the amount of context and engagement with superhero comics is dependent on how far a person wants to go with a pre-existing narrative.

How many times do you think that people have been reading their first *Batman* comic and came across a reference to a previous case, or character, and felt a pull to find out what that reference meant, who that person is that is being referenced, or the alternate story line that supports the reference? Odds are that people at least curious enough to do a little bit of digging into the past of these characters and the universes they inhabit. Such curiosities can be assisted by using a form of historical criticism. The goal of using historical criticism in reading superhero comics is not to diminish the enjoyment, rather, it is to explore areas that one might not have previously considered.

The historical criticism I draw from in evaluating superhero comics comes from Latrobe and Drury's (2009) book *Critical Approaches to Young Adult Literature*. In it, a basic outline of historical criticism is presented as a malleable set of guiding questions concerning different areas of inquiry.

Chronological Considerations

Superhero comics are normally in some sort of serialized form. That serialization can take place daily, weekly, monthly, etc, depending upon the creator or publishers. Superhero comics are, as writer Jonathan Hickman has described in writing monthly comics at Marvel, stories that are in a "perpetual second act". Essentially what Hickman is describing are stories that are rooted in a continual rising action where they must problem solve to beat the antagonizing force of the moment. To apply historical criticism, you need to look at the story arc, or, the collected arcs of multiple stories that are presented in trade books. For example, a trade paperback collects the what typically amounts to four to six issues from a comics series in order to tell a complete, stand alone story or what is also known as an "arc." These arcs, when taken together, make up the ongoing story of the characters involved in that series. One can then take a trade paperback from a superhero series and apply historical criticism by asking the following regarding chronology:

Is there an importance about the time the book was written? Serialized superhero books are built in chunks of three-to-five issues to tell one story arc, so does the collection contribute significantly to a recent set of stories? Does it tie into a larger crossover event, such as a *Secret Wars* or *Flashpoint*? When considering chronology the word continuity creeps up in writings and conversations about comics and for good reason. Superhero universes are built on the events that have come in the past, the future, and even alternate universes.

Content and Setting

Gotham, Metropolis, the New York City of the 616-universe of Marvel heroes. These are all very specific places where the action of so many stories in a shared superhero universe take place. For many who have spent any amount of time in these fictional places, the cities that have such amazing protectors can become a character unto itself. When evaluating superhero comics ask yourself the following regarding setting and content:

Is the setting (time, place, circumstance) important to the story overall? Could it have been anytime, anyplace? Is that appropriate? While these seem like no-brainer questions, they do have great impact when thinking about the quality of the story overall. For example, in Grant Morrison's massive run on *Batman*, he incorporated a number of chronologically daring storytelling over a large amount of monthly or even bimonthly titles. The problem can be, in these instances, that books come out of order due to production schedules, or even, the publisher may not help the reader by providing the proper chronological order of titles.

Is there any factual or fictional history that is presented? Regarding superhero comics, this question directly speaks to continuity. For the heroes that save the universe time and time again over the decades, the timelines, stories, and events can become muddled. Since the mid 1980s' the major publishers such as DC comics and Marvel have reset their continuity, devising grand story lines that reveal alternate histories and universes. Keeping up with continuity in a historical context in the 21st century is much easier than it has been in the past with the internet and various wikis that have been created to help promote certain characters and stories.

Author Context

The people who create these adventures are hard working creative people. As most creative writing teachers will tell you (I having helmed my share of creative writing classroom activities personally can attest to this), you try to fold some aspects of yourself, something about your own likes, fears, joys, and pains, you own fantasies and tangible experiences into the things that you are trying to write. Trying to ascertain the influences and motives of an author, however, is an area of caution in using historical criticism, and one I want to address. When you set out on the road of finding the context an author may or may not be supplying to the work, keep in mind the following two points: Don't assume for sure that the context informed the author; and, don't take the author's word at face value alone. With that in mind, when evaluating superhero comics ask yourself the following regarding author context:

Does the body of work of the author influence anything about the work? More and more it is rare for any one creator or creative team to work on one main superhero title for more than a handful of years. Recent exceptions include Scott Snyder and Greg Capullo's *Batman*, however, such lengthy runs open an opportunity to ask how the author has has created something with a set of characters over a significant time period. In the case of *Batman,* there is a concrete origin story in place in what many would consider is the "main" universe, i.e., Bruce Wayne's parents are killed in front of him putting him on the path to become Batman. But how does Snyder put himself, his own experiences in life and reading *Batman,* to use in the stories he creates? Internet research of interviews with the author can help lead to asking questions about the life of the author as they have worked on the book. Was there a tragedy in their life that influenced a storyline? Was there something occurring in the world that found it's way somehow into the storylines?

What I found in listening to interviews with Scott Snyder on podcasts like *Imaginary Worlds* (2015) was he was a comics fan who grew up in New York City and was drawn to the resiliency of the character of Batman. Snyder grew up reading, like many comics book fans who came of age in the 1980s', the violent Dark Knight shaped by Frank Miller in tiles like *Year One* and *The Dark*

Knight Returns. Even with that influence Snyder moves his writing in the opposite direction of Miller and strives to explore his own anxieties, fears, and hopes. Even though Snyder talks about how he wanted to write Batman as if he had no known history, the stories, the mythology he is trying to create folds into the overall continuity in a seemingly natural way, as if his stories have always been there in the Batman universe. In a sense, Snyder has created his own continuity, one that now folds into the larger DC universe.

Time Capsule

Serialized superhero comics do tend to reflect the times they are created, but that is no different than any other media. In a positive light, the adaptation of characters to reflect the issues or trends of a time period help to bring in new readers, to invite new ideas into the conversations people share about a character or story. In superhero comics there is a unique opportunity for massive generational sharing. For example, those who grew up in the 70s' reading *Superman* can share experiences and feelings about the story arcs and character with those reading *Superman* in the 21st century. The very nature of mainstream superhero stories (e.g., Superman, Batman, Captain America), in a historical context are the stories are not really static. You have to think of these stories not as you think of a novel. Superhero stories, no matter the time period, remain malleable with every story arc, every new creative team, as the overall story of who the people inhabiting the universe changes a little bit more. When evaluating superhero comics ask yourself the following regarding the time period a comic is created within:

Is the work a cultural time capsule? Was it intended for a specific audience at a specific time? If so, has the audience changed, and, if so, has that changed the way the work is received? Also, think about does the time period reflect certain storytelling elements of the time, or fads? For example, is there a significant number of Batman titles and collections released the same year a new major motion picture is released?

Conclusion

Walk into any comic book shop and pluck an issue of *Batman*, *Iron Man*, or any of the dozens of superhero titles published regularly and you will find yourself in the middle of a much larger, ongoing story that realistically began before you were probably old enough to read comics. This does not diminish the enjoyment that can come in reading stories of these heroes and heroines, rather, it is an opportunity to jump into a universe and build on a rich historical past that is always looking for more pages, more chapters, more conversations to occur.

Works Cited

Latrobe, Kathy Howard, and Judy Drury. *Critical approaches to young adult literature*. Neal Schuman Pub, 2009.

Molinsky, Eric. "Being Batman". *Imaginary Worlds,* http://www.imaginaryworldspodcast.org/being-batman--for-now--1.html

Sims, Chris. "Jonathan Hickman and the Mad Science of 'The Manhattan Projects' [Interview]". http://comicsalliance.com/jonathan-hickman-and-the-mad-science-of-the-manhattan-projects/

Concerns of the Critic

Critiquing comics takes a certain amount of care regardless of whether the published piece will be for a grade in class or on a major news website. The following articles focus on ways academics and reviewers alike can better nuance their analyses in order to provide a clear, fair, and balanced discussion about their respective subjects of interest.

Every Word Counts: Long-Form vs. Short-Form Critiques

by Christine Atchison

It is an exciting time to be reviewing and analyzing comics; the field is new enough that there is plenty of ground to be covered yet is established enough that there are, to echo an observation I made in 2014 that rings with a growing truth, "a number of thoughtful monographs, edited collections, and articles focusing on the form, history, impact, distinctiveness, reception, and effects of comics."[1] The variety of topics that have been covered by scholars (and fans!) speak to what I find most inspiring about comics themselves: their many genres, formal innovations, and adaptations across a variety of media (film and video games quickly come to mind) require truly interdisciplinary approaches.

That said, there is so much to cover and so many ways to do it that the potential of comics can, and seems to have, become a bit of a double-edged sword. There are far too many reviews and analyses that are either much too long or not nearly long enough to accomplish what the author's aim appears to be. It is very easy to either try to cover everything there is about a particular comics-oriented subject or – to borrow an old adage my professors used to warn me with – to miss the forest for the trees and neglect entire planes of meaning. Both errors seem to suggest a lack of formal medium-specific knowledge and organization and both end in the same result: poor reviews and analyses that are either unwieldy, incomplete, unbalanced, or a combination of the three.

Comics: The Meaty Medium that Requires a Specialized Recipe

Serious comic reviews and analyses are a relatively new phenomenon that correspond with the recent encroachment of comics into territory traditionally reserved for so-called "high art." As a result, far too many reviewers and

---

[1] Christine Atchison, "Religion, Popular Culture, and the Myths of Historical and Political Secularity" in *Religião, mídia e cultura*, eds. Iuri Andréas Reblin and Júlio Cézar Adam (São Leopoldo, Brasil: Faculdades EST, 2015), 228.

scholars seem to treat comics like some of their cultural counterparts – especially film and more traditional literature. The impulse to borrow from film and literature studies when reviewing or analyzing comics is not surprising and is not entirely harmful (comics often involve both image and text, so it makes sense to borrow from scholars who have textual and image expertise); it can, however, become counterproductive when solely text or image-based methodologies are applied without modification.

Most reviews aimed at a non-academic audience will not require dipping into the theory behind how formal aspects of comics affect readers and reading. That said, it is helpful to have a basic understanding of some of these theories and formal aspects to be better able to reflect upon and write about the way comic medial traits (especially the interplay between text and images) are used by artists and writers to subvert or bring a narrative (or even a genre), to life.[2]

The sometimes conflict-ridden relationship between image and text may find its roots in antiquity but it continues to be consistently revisited in debates about how comics should be discussed today.[3] Comics practitioner-turned-theorist Scott McCloud, for instance, claims that comics are at once neither and both art and writing: they are, for him, their own language.[4] While McCloud's

---

[2] I highly recommend owning a few good supplementary guides that draw attention to the many formal aspects of comics not mentioned in this chapter. Scott McCloud's work has been highly criticized, but is still a great jumping off point as it is organized, thorough, and accessible for reviewers who are unable dive more deeply into comic theories. The two I would most highly recommend as starting reference points are *Understanding Comics* (Northampton: Tundra Publishing, 1993) and *Making Comics* (New York: Harper, 2006). Neil Cohn's work is also worth a look. It is more theory-laden than McCloud's and tends to focus on the grammar of comics – so it will not be for everyone – but it is groundbreaking and is a great entry-point if you are a fan of linguistics. You can find a list of his work (including many free articles) on his website: www.visuallanguagelab.com/vloc.html. Will Eisner has also released quite helpful guides: Will Eisner, *Comics and Sequential Art: Principals and Practices from the Legendary Cartoonist* (Tamarac, FL: Poorhouse Press, 1985); Will Eisner, *Graphic Storytelling and Visual Narrative: Principals and Practices from the Legendary Cartoonist* (Tamarac, FL: Poorhouse Press, 1996).

[3] For more on how an image vs. words mentality may have begun with Plato see Shahira Fahmy, Mary Angela Bock, and Wayne Wanta, *Visual Communication Theory and Research: A Mass Communication Perspective* (New York: Palgrave Macmillan, 2014), 8.

[4] Scott McCloud, *Understanding Comics* (William Morrow Paperbacks, 1994), 17.

statement seems to suggest that he gives equal weight to both image and text, his collective work tends to privilege image over text. He even defines comics as "…pictorial and other images in deliberate sequences intended to convey information and/or to produce an aesthetic response in the viewer."[5] Thomas E. Wartenberg, in an article that sometimes opposes and sometimes echoes McCloud, claims that "it is characteristic of comics to give equal priority to the text and the pictures" going so far as to state that, in comics, "…neither the text nor the image provides an independent constraint upon the other."[6]

Debates surrounding the primacy of images and text in comics are likely to continue. Regardless of which side you choose (if any), the important thing to remember when reviewing comics is that they are a medium in and of themselves (not a genre!), whose definition tends to center around the relationship between image and text. To focus on just one of these core aspects constitutes a gross oversight. At this point I would be remiss if I didn't address comics that are created with "just" text or "just" images: leaving out a core medial-element is often purposeful and worth examination when an author chooses to do so, meaning that even if the textual aspect, for instance, of a comic is missing it is still worth commenting on.

Though the building blocks of comics are often words and images, they are much more than that, making a simple combination of textual and image analysis a poor approach. The grammar of film and literature studies is useful for studying comics as they share some of the same features (framing, *mise en scene*, characterization, narrative composition, etc.), but many of these elements operate differently in a comic than they may in a film, book, or even a motion comic.

Take, for instance, filmic shots and comic panels: a still frame from a film in drawn form would, at first, look very similar to a comic panel, but they are not the same thing. Just as a photograph is not the same thing as a painting, even if the painting is created in such a way that it looks identical to a photograph: "We might say: 'A painting *is* a world; a photograph is *of* a world.'"[7] Both the

---

[5] Scott McCloud, *Understanding Comics* (William Morrow Paperbacks, 1994), 9.

[6] Thomas E. Wartenberg, "Wordy Pictures: Theorizing the Relationship between Image and Text in Comics," in *The Art of Comics: A Philosophical Approach*, eds. Aaron Meskin and Roy T Cook (Chichester: Blackwell Publishing Ltd.), 87.

[7] Stanley Cavell, qtd. in Burke Hilsabeck, "The 'Is' in *What Is Cinema*?: On André Bazin and Stanley Cavell," *Cinema Journal* 55, no. 2 (2016): 33. Original source:

still frame and the comic panel may indicate a moment in time, but – to borrow another one of McCloud's claims – *"unlike* other media, in comics, the past is more than just *memories* for the audience, and the future is more than just *possibilities!* Both past and future are *real* and *visible* and *all around us."* Because "space does for comics what time does for film," comics, unlike other media, are able to show many places (even worlds) and timelines simultaneously on one page.[8] The way comics treat panels, time, space, setting, and characters support Roy T. Cook's suggestion that "comics allow for more complex structural relationships between 'units' than can be reproduced in film."[9]

It should also be noted that comics have features that are wholly unique and further enable them to communicate narratives in ways unavailable to either film or literature – meaning any analysis of comics should account for these unique attributes. The most obvious comics-only feature is the gutter, a space that Evan Thomas argues "contributes an entire plane of meaning to comics that employ it."[10] Scott McCloud comments on the importance of the gutter when he suggests that it creates a space for the reader to be a sort-of co-creator – they have to fill in the blanks and become more invested in the narrative as a result. Douglas Rushkoff seems to echo McCloud's claim when he argues that "a comic requires a leap of faith from its readers every time they move from one panel to the next."[11] McCloud would call Rushkoff's "leap of faith" an example of closure (the "phenomenon of observing the parts but perceiving the whole"), and argues that part of the effectiveness of comics as a

---

Stanley Cavell, *The World Viewed: Reflections on the Ontology of Film* (Cambridge: Harvard University Press, 1979). A more in depth painting vs. photograph illustration (written by Hilsabeck) can also be found on this page.

[8] Scott McCloud, *Understanding Comics* (William Morrow Paperbacks, 1994), 7.

[9] Roy T. Cook, "Why Comics are not Films: Metacomics and Medium-Specific Conventions," in *The Art of Comics: A Philosophical Approach*, eds. Aaron Meskin and Roy T Cook (Chichester: Blackwell Publishing Ltd.), 171.

[10] Evan Thomas, "Invisible Art, Invisible Planes, Invisible People," in *Multicultural Comics: From Zap to Blue Beetle*, ed. Frederick Luis Aldama (Austin: University of Texas Press, 2010), 156.

[11] Douglas Rushkoff, "Foreword: Looking for God in the Gutter," in *Graven Images: Religion in Comic Books and Graphic Novels*, eds. A. David Lewis ad Christine Hoff Kraemer (New York: Continuum, 2010), x.

medium lays in their ability to use "closure like no other."[12] An overview of all the aspects of the comics medium that make it unique is beyond the scope of this section – that would require far more than one chapter! – but what I hope to have demonstrated is that comics are a unique medium that require a unique methodology and a healthy dose of economical writing and focus if one is to review or analyze them.

Okay, Comics Have Unique Medial Conventions: Now What?

The question of when to write a short-form review and when to write a long-form review will depend on what your aim is, who your audience is, what is important to said audience, and whether or not you have a word count. As your knowledge of comics increases, so too will the temptation to share everything that you know. Although medium-specific comics knowledge is paramount, it should only be addressed when it directly relates to the aim or theme of your review. If, for instance, the review is for an art-oriented blog, an increased focus on color, line, brush/pen/marker work, lettering, page layout, and other relevant elements and principles of art within the works should be addressed. The textual elements should never be ignored, but extending the length of your review to address them in the same depth when the audience is looking for an art-centered review would not be wise. Reviewing comics is a balancing act: it is important not to overlook any element that may relate to the aim of the review without getting lost by trying to address every element equally unless your word-count allows for it and the audience expects it.

Keep Your Friends Close and Your Audience Closer

Knowing your audience means a lot more than knowing what they expect: you should know that they may not be like you and may not read a comic the way you do. In practice, this means allowing room for productive discussion about your review and remembering that texts are not autonomous.[13] They do

---

[12] Scott McCloud, *Understanding Comics* (William Morrow Paperbacks, 1994), 63-65.

[13] For more on the autonomy of the text please see: Roland Barthes, "The Death of the Author," (1967); Will Brooker, *Hunting the Dark Knight: Twenty-First Century Batman* (London: IB Taurus, 2012); Paul Ricoeur, *From Text to Action: Essays in Hermeneutics, II*, trans. J. B. Thompson (Evanston Illinois: Northwestern University Press, 2007); Michel Foucault, "What Is an Author?," in *Aesthetics, Method, and Epistomology*, eds. James D. Faubion (The New Press,), 205–222.

not stand alone and they do not carry ingrained meanings; they "can only mean something in the context of the experience and situation of [their] particular audience."[14] Put differently, texts are open to a number of interpretations and many of "these interpretations will depend on the viewer or reader's membership of some specific cultural communities."[15] Texts written out of certain cultural communities tend to assume cultural familiarity and can sometimes support stereotypes common within that culture. When the content of a review allows it, you may want to take advantage of a great opportunity to interrogate the cultural assumptions found within the comic and connect your review to real-world issues.

Knowing your audience might also mean knowing what kinds of readers they are: if they are unlikely to be very familiar with comics you may have to allot space for defining terms (like the gutter I discussed earlier). If your audience is likely to know some comics jargon you may be able to save some of your precious word-count to address other related issues. Jargon, by the way, does not have to be an enemy; when it is well used it can improve a review. That said, using jargon (or overly complicated prose for that matter) in lieu of simpler words (or sentence structures) can end up making your review unwieldy and difficult to read. If a review ends up being quite long, does not use too much jargon or overly complicated language, and still seems unwieldy, some signposting may be necessary to keep your reader on track (and please note that signposting is not the same as repetition!). Lastly, if your review is getting a bit too long and you notice it involves many descriptive paragraphs, it may be time to recall that comics combine text and images and so should your review! A picture is worth a thousand words after all.

Putting it all Together

The key to knowing when (and how) to write a short- or long-form review begins with doing your research (learning about the comics medium so that your reviewer/analyzer utility belt contains the tools necessary to address what

---

[14] Lawrence Grossberg, "Is There a Fan in the House?: The Affective Sensibility of Fandom," in *The Adoring Audience: Fan Culture and Popular Media*, ed. Lisa A Lewis (London: Routledge, 1992), 53.
[15] Will Brooker and Deborah Jermyn, "Introduction to 'Part Seven – Interpretive Communities: Nation and Ethnicity,'" in *The Audience Studies Reader*, eds. Will Brooker and Deborah Jermyn (London: Routledge, 2003), 275.

is important to you and your readers) and knowing your audience. After you have determined your aims and your audience's expectations you can begin to structure a review that fits the task. Knowing the medium will help you to understand which formal aspects will require more attention than others and which will be beyond your scope. Knowing your audience will help you to know what you need to cover, how you need to cover it, and what jargon is or is not acceptable. When these tips are combined with a philosophy of economy and a recognition of the power of a well-placed figure, you should be able to create a review for any occasion!

Comics and Context: The Questions That Must Be Asked

by A. David Lewis

You have a blindspot.

More literally, you likely have two, given a pair of healthy, functioning eyes. All the photoreceptors in your retina collect at one point, then the optic nerve travels from there to your brain. At that collection area, though, there are no receptors themselves, so the brain must compensate, filling in, without your even noticing, subtle colors or patterns to complete your vision. In effect, you can never *see* your blindspot; your mind hides it from you.

Similarly, in your comics criticism and reviews, you likely have a blindspot – only one if you're lucky, but potentially far more. It's not your fault, of course. The latest comic book out in shops comes after decades in the making, with the history, economics, politics, and personalities of a professional industry, not to mention a whole nation, informing it. The critic is only at fault if he or she ignores the possibility of such a blindspot or bias: one's only sin would be that of presuming infallibility.

Therefore, context is key, both your own and that of the work you're examining. Of course, you cannot incorporate all of world history and global thought into, say, a 500-word review, yet a critic still needs to properly anchor his or her reading of comic so that it's neither oblivious to context nor only of the moment. A surgical approach is needed, one that both acknowledges your blindspot and unlocks the work being covered in a way your readers could not expect.

In turn, these are the questions that must be asked.

What is your own bias concerning the work or its subject matter?

Loosely speaking, *heteronormativity* is the assumption, conscious or otherwise, that male-female pairings are the natural basis for a culture. The word "natural" is worth emphasizing here, because many who actively support the heteronormative viewpoint point to the animal kingdom as innately supporting their case. That only works, though, if they conveniently ignore all same-sex behaviors demonstrated by animals. As with anything that claims to be "normal," heteronormativity is a construction – just an idea or a social rule, something created by human society.

So, connected to the natural world or not, societies do not necessarily operate in cleanly heteronormative systems, nor might narratives. This is among the first element in *identity politics* that should be interrogated when engaging a comic. Do either you as the critic or the comic as a product favor a particularly status, creed, or political viewpoint? This can span from LGBTQI matters to racial bias to misogyny or misandry. And, of course, it can spill into the religious realm, either as obviously pernicious as anti-semitism or Islamophobia or more subtle, as in atheophobia or rampant secularism.

Stop to question your own agenda before preparing to analyze the comic's. We all have biases, after all, and they cannot be avoided. They don't need to be avoided, only acknowledged – they can even be usefully utilized. Though the story may be set on an alien planet or foreign land, to what degree might *Americentrism* or the presumption of a democratic ideal play a role? Likewise, while storytelling itself may be universal, narrative methods differ from one culture to the next: What manner of "heroism" is presented as the norm here? Moreover, what constitutes morality either in the world of the comic or that of the comic creators? Have they created a *narrative structure* here that their audiences would easily recognize (e.g. conflict, rising action, climax, denouement) or are they presenting a challenge in their method of storytelling?

How is this not a work from any other medium but comics?

Nearly all of the questions above could be asked of any medium, but, in terms of comics, there is the special *hybridity* of word and image that needs particular consideration. That is, while comics can employ a three-act structure, for instance, the same as film or epic poem, it has its own varieties of medium-based structures for narrative. Is the story more art-driven than word-driven? Do the collaborators involved seem to be, figuratively and literally speaking, on the same page? Or, might the writer be scripting for an artist who was only later selected? Having a sensitivity to any (mis)balance benefits the critic nearly as much as determining the work's value.

Let's say that word and image, impressively, are blending together nicely: the additional influences and expectations of *genre* demand attention. Just as the space ranger and his mores would be quite out of place in the environment of a Victorian novel, elements that are expected, innovative, or simply misaligned with the *genre conventions* of a work need to be detected by the critique. This is true several times over for the comic book critic: First, is the presumed dominant superhero genre exerting an influence on the work? Second, keep that hybridity in mind again. Do the images or layouts or even the lettering match the genre expectations? Does the text do the same and to the same degree? Before merging them back together, looking at the implementation of *visual genre* and *textual genre* separately can aid in clarifying how overall genre functions for the work. Does it, ultimately, abide by genre or does it counter audience expectations of the genre (either by deconstructing them – intentionally breaking down their rules for greater insights – or by renegotiating them)?

One additional wrinkle to the comic book is its frequent use of *seriality*. Of course, comics are not the only medium to employ this system of connected, episodic stories; soap operas, movie serials, and even Dickensian novels frequently operate in the same fashion. Moreover, the rise of the so-called graphic novel has disrupted assumptions about seriality for the medium. Therefore, a critic needs to put in context whether the work in question is "one and done," is reliant on other installments to inform its narrative, or is operating in an even more complicated system of intertextuality – what, for the main superhero publishers, is frequently called *continuity*. This relationship with seriality (not to be confused with *sequence*, the building block of comics' panel associations) will, likewise, impact how genre is deployed: Does the comic book move from one genre to the next, does it borrow from other genres via continuity, or does it dissociate from other texts (perhaps by the same publisher, but not necessarily) by engaging in distinct genre conventions?

What is the work's message?

In theory, all works – comics or otherwise – have a message... even if that message is, paradoxically, "This has no message." Outside of absolute mercenary employment (for which the message could still be, "This was done for money"), all art has a *raison d'etre*: a reason for being. That reason could be as basic as providing entertainment and perhaps escapism; these are not, despite the pejorative use of the word "escapist" in some context, unworthy goals by themselves. A comic can be made – in fact, some comics *need* to be made – purely for an audience's enjoyment and as a brief reprieve from their everyday lives.

However, a critic cannot make the *a priori* assumption that the work in question must be motivated either by money or for entertainment value without investigating further. Certainly, in addition to the work's narrative, the *tone* of both its art and its text will provide the most salient clues for any potential agenda being pursued. Could the comic be read in a *satirical* fashion? Could it be understood in a *political* framework? Could it be taken as some form of *evangelical*? Might it have a *personal* impetus by its creator(s)? Does it make, overtly or furtively, any *industrial* claims, taking issue with the business apparatus to which it is tied?

A work's message need not necessarily be negative, but, most often, the more jarring and disruptive the message, the more covert it needs to be. In fact, it is those messages most contrary to the real-life *status quo* of the reader and the comics industry that will commonly require the most decoding by a critic. How are the story's tone, environment, characters, and narrative intended to affect real-life *hegemony*, the power structures that largely control the audience's world?

And, add to this both a *market-dependent* lens. That is, for whom is such a message intended, in what time period, and across what geographies? A message targeting one particular space and time can take on new meaning and new significance at a later date or to an outside community. When reviewing *manga* translated for an American, English-speaking market, for example, you need some cognizance of a shift in the messaging – all the moreso if it's decades-old reprint!

Against what backdrop is this work being produced?

All of the aforementioned questions operate against two distinct backdrops. The first is the context of the producer. That is, what has gone into the production of this comic? Beyond the paper, the ink, the shipping, and the distribution, what *corporate* aspects should inform your critique? The publisher in question might be a new and rising force or it might be teetering on the edge of bankruptcy; if it's a small press or self-published, the story behind their enterprise may be more informative than the comic itself. Recalling the warnings of Americentrism, the critic has to consider whether this is a domestic, foreign, or collaboratively international work – with all the cultural baggage any one of those might carry (e.g. religiosity, politics, trade, etc.). Even the season in which a work is produced and then released, the current events operating in the background, may have a salient effect on the comic at hand.

Though it's convenient to lay the entirety of a work at one primary creator's feet, that impulse needs to be checked much of the time. Discussing, to offer one case, "Alan Moore's *Watchmen*" entirely overlooks the contributions of Dave Gibbons, of John Higgins, of their editors, and of the wider DC Comics production, marketing, and distribution teams. Even in the case of 'auteur' works (e.g. Art Spiegelman's *MAUS* or Kate Beaton's *Hark! A Vagrant*), critics who center on the intent or personality of an author run counter to the arguments of literary theorists like Roland Barthes or Michel Foucault; they suggest that the work itself is the primary concern, not some disconnected, distant, absent author. Talking about a comic in terms of what its author thinks or intended is, at best, speculation and, at worst, fantasy.

Of course, as noted earlier, one cannot know everything: geopolitics changes by the day, and the history of the comics medium stretches back at least to Richard Occault (d. 1928) if not Rudolphe Töpffer (d. 1846) or even further, to ancient Egyptian hieroglyphics! The key here isn't in knowing everything. The key is in knowing what might be relevant and, more importantly, knowing what you do not know. Putting your review or analysis in a defined context not only safeguards you from unforeseen, undermining trivia (e.g. "But doesn't that panel refer to the 1940 trade unions?"), but it also gives your readers a solid frame. An acknowledgment of your parameters as a critique relieves undue burden on you and helps direct your readers. Therefore, in terms of the producer's context, you must ask: what geographical, historical, and cultural timeframe should be placed within the parameters of the review?

Who is invested in this work?

The second major backdrop against which to consider a comic is the context of the consumer. And, of course, similar questions apply: Is this meant for a domestic audience, a foreign audience, or a global audience? How wide a distribution net does it have? Is it affordable to readers or does it require an atypical financial investment? What level of education is presumed for the audience?

However, the consumer's context has some additional layers that too often go overlooked. First, there is the figurative echo chamber between the context of the publisher and the context of the consumer. For instance, what is considered expert work by one publisher in the eyes of readers might be considered trash in terms of the reader's expectations for other publishers. The stark and stylized approach of Marjane Satrapi in producing *Persepolis* might be misperceived as unskilled or childish if it was found in between the covers of a Marvel comic. Likewise, the superhero style of someone like Jim Lee could be mistaken as juvenile or cartoonish to an art house comics publisher like Drawn & Quarterly. Overall, though a comic might make demands of an audience to which it was not accustomed: more violence, greater nuance, more elaborate art, etc. The consumer and the producer's expectations of each other shift and blur with every week, even if one is considering an individual consumer and a self-published mini-comic producer. Large or small, there is a *feedback loop* in the comics field that is far tighter than might be found for other, mass-produced media, and it cannot go overlooked.

More generally, though, comics endures the same double-edged sword as most other consumer media, namely the potential gap between the *intended/target audience* and the *buying readership*. Could the Vertigo imprint in its early days have possibly suspected that *Sandman* would pick up a following in the LGBTQ community? And the publisher Houghton Mifflin likely didn't think of Broadway enthusiasts in its original demographic plan for *Fun Home*'s first release. In some cases, the gap is minimal or even inclusive, with, for instance, a comic being aimed at teenage boys and, instead, it is bought by both boys and girls from their teens into their college years. The trouble lies with a work presumed for a target it does not hit or, perhaps worse, finding an unwelcome demographic. For years, the working (mis)assumption was that superhero comics were for teen males; hard *data*, though, does not support that – both the age-group and, in many cases, the sex of the readership was in conflict with the "conventional wisdom." (And look out here for that heteronormativity and any gender binary that might be underlying either the data or the target!) An interpretation of a work might change radically when, instead of the comic being purchased for tween girls with messages about emotional intelligence and compassion, it is ravenously consumed by adult-aged men with murky sexual overtones. Does the publisher cater to their mistargeted-yet-successful demo? Do creators approach the work the same way? Do they adhere to the original message?

What's your blindspot?

By asking the essential questions provided in this chapter, critics may be able to unlock deeper readings of the work and, in turn, guide readers to its greater importance. Informing the reader is only half the job of a critic, regardless of medium: challenging the reader to see larger patterns is the aim – and the responsibility – of a seasoned reviewer, whatever the medium.

Underrepresentation, Stereotyping, Objectification, and Plot Devices: Female Characters in Superhero Comics

by Carolyn Cocca

Female superhero characters have historically been much less numerous, much more often stereotyped, much more often sexualized, and much less likely to drive the action than their male counterparts. This began in earnest after the Second World War, when women were forced out of "men's" jobs and into a "cult of domesticity" in which the male was the breadwinning patriarch of the nuclear family, and the female the wife and mother in a secondary role. While the Second and Third Waves of feminism made some headway in subverting this gender binary and its inequalities, backlash against feminist ideas pushed for more "traditional" gendered depictions at the same time. In the 1990s and 2000s in particular, the comics industry was heavily reliant on sales through local comic shops, which fostered a narrower fan base (older, male, white, heterosexual) and a smaller number of female characters who were more objectified and more violent. This improved somewhat in the 2010s, as certain segments of a broadened fanbase pushed for change through convention attendance, social media, and directing their dollars toward new titles starring more diverse and multifaceted female characters.

In general, though, superhero comics tend to exhibit certain trends in their depictions of female characters:

Underrepresentation

Women are, of course, half the population of Earth, but they are greatly underrepresented not only in positions of power but also across fiction. The number of superhero comics starring women is extremely low. Even lower are the number of superhero comics that have an equal number of males and females on a team, or the number that have an equal number of male and female characters overall.

First, consider whether a given comic book is a title starring a male character like Captain America, a title starring a female character like Black

Widow, or a title starring an ensemble like the Avengers. Note the writer and artist of the book, the publisher of the book, how many female-headed titles they are publishing, and how many of those female-headed titles are written and/or drawn by women. How diverse are that publisher's titles and their writers and artists overall? The percentage of mainstream superhero comics starring female characters is at a high of about 12%, and the percentage of mainstream superhero comics written or drawn by women is about the same.[16] These numbers differ by publisher and change slightly from month to month.

Second, is there a female character on the team at all, or is there only one, or is there more than one? On superhero teams, there are usually one or two females among several males. For instance, the Justice League consists of six men and Wonder Woman. An *Avengers* title or an *X-Men* title might have one or perhaps two or three women on the team. If there is more than one female character on the team, do they look similar to or different from one another?

Third, look at how many of the characters in the book are female versus male overall. In a sample of comics from the mid-1990s, mid-2000s, and mid-2010s, I found that female characters were about 40% of all characters in female-headed titles and about 25% of all characters in ensemble titles (Cocca 2014a). The number in male-headed titles is probably similar to that of the ensemble titles, or perhaps even lower. For all three types of books, note the types of ads in the book, note whose letters are published in the letter column in the back (if there is one), and note what the book's creators are saying about it on social media. The ads, letters, and tweets, along with the centrality and number of female characters, point toward who the assumed audience for the book is.

After establishing the numbers, give the book the three-part Bechdel-Wallace test:[17] are there at least two female characters who speak to one another about something other than a man? This is a very low bar, but many books fail it. And since female characters are so few in number, they must each carry heavy narrative weight, standing in for "all" females such that their characterizations assume heightened importance.

---

[16] Cocca 2016.

[17] This is more commonly called the "Bechdel" test. But Alison Bechdel herself prefers "Bechdel-Wallace" as the test was first articulated by her friend Liz Wallace. Wallace is thanked in the first panel in the original comic strip in which the test appears (see Bechdel 1985).

Stereotypes and Diversity

Note whether the female characters written or drawn as *stereotypes* of women: supportive, emotional, tied to home and children, out-of-control, a damsel-in-distress. Are they central to the plot or are they more supportive of male characters driving the plot? Are they more interested in romance than the male characters, particularly, in opposite-sex romance? Are they shown working, or in the home, or with children? Are they nagging the male characters? Are they drawn in the middle of a superhero group, or leading the group, or are they more to the side? Are they unable to control their emotions or their powers? Do they get depowered by a villain, or due to a mistake they themselves have made? Do they require rescue from the male characters? Are any of the male characters portrayed in these ways?

If there are two or more women, are they *diverse*? In general, female superhero characters are usually white, heterosexual, upper-middle-class, able-bodied, and attractive by white Anglo-European standards. Note how many of them fit this description, how many do not, and how they do not. Because of the underrepresentation of female characters, if there is only one female character, and she does fit this description, it contributes to media erasure of all other women.

In terms of *race or ethnicity or national origin*, are white females more central to the action than females of color, or more powerful than females of color? Are the females of color exoticized, in terms of dress or powers? Black female superheroes historically have been even more sexualized than their white counterparts, and are more likely to have animalistic powers. For instance, Vixen is often drawn with a physics-defying plunging neckline, and her power comes from an African totem worn around her neck that enables her to channel the strengths of any animal.[18] Are the black women in the story caregiving "mammies," or sexy "Jezebels," or angry "Sapphires"?[19] Do they have natural hair, or is it relaxed? Female East Asian superheroes or supervillains might fall into submissive "china doll," or sexy "geisha girl," or mysterious "dragon lady" stereotypes.[20] Are they martial arts experts who are then bested by a white male character? South Asian female characters may be written as

---

[18] Brown 2013.
[19] West 2008.
[20] Prasso 2005.

"model minorities." Middle Eastern female characters may be written as focused on Islam or somehow linked with terrorism. Overall, are female characters of color written with complexity and care? That there is probably only one such character, if any, again means that she must stand in for all females matching her demographic characteristics.

Are there any LGBTQ characters in the book? Are they written with their *gender or sexuality* as the main feature of their characterization, or as one aspect of it? Are they having difficulty "accepting" their gender and/or sexuality? Are they shown with a significant other or always alone? These same four questions can be applied to characters with *disabilities* as well. Further, is the disabled character a "super-crip" whom everyone admires for "moving past" their disability and achieving great things, or does s/he have some superpower or prosthesis that excessively counterbalances the disability? Are the queer or disabled bodies drawn much differently from those of the non-queer, non-disabled bodies? Are they more sexualized or less sexualized?[21]

Objectification and Sexualization

Female bodies, like male bodies in superhero comics, are often portrayed as super-strong. Both types of bodies have been idealized and objectified in superhero comics, and in quite exaggerated ways.

However, the idealization and objectification are not at all the same. In short, female bodies are almost always very *sexualized* in ways their male counterparts are not. From the 1990s in particular, also known as the "Bad Girl" era of comic art, the male characters were generally drawn facing front, fully clothed, with a focus on their musculature and power. The females were drawn more often from the side, in much skimpier clothing, with a focus on their "T&A." Male bodies were athleticized and strong; female bodies were sexualized and submissive. There was simply no equivalent focus on males' primary or secondary sex characteristics. Much of this style of art, and its gendered binaries, lingers today.

First, note what the female characters are wearing compared to what the male characters are wearing. How much skin are they showing? Are they spilling out of their clothes? If someone were wearing those clothes in real life, would it require magic to hold her "t" or "a" inside the fabric? Are any male

---

[21] Cocca 2014b.

characters showing skin or scantily clad? Are the females wearing "women's" clothes and the males wearing "men's" clothes, or are some of the characters wearing clothes traditionally associated with the other – if so, is this used for comic effect, or is it part of the character's usual dress?

Second, note how the female characters are posed compared to how the male characters are posed. See if they pass the *Broke Back Test*: Are the females posed in such a way that you can see both curves of their behind and both of their breasts at the same time, such that their back would have to be broken to hold that position? (Cocca 2014a). Does their posing bring attention more to their sexuality than their athleticism, or more to their curves than their strength? Are only parts of their bodies in some panels; particularly, without their face being shown? Are their powers more of the "pose and point" variety, or are they engaged in hand-to-hand action? Are any male characters posed in these ways? Objectification of characters generally means that the reader is looking "at" them rather than identifying with them or looking "through" their eyes. Those characters' stories are not being told and their power is subverted.

Centrality to the Plot and Use of Plot Devices

Keeping in mind how a given female character is drawn along with her contribution to the story as a whole, give the book what comics writer Kelly Sue DeConnick calls the "Sexy Lamp test": is the female character so superfluous to the action that she could be replaced with a sexy lamp and the plot would still function? (Hudson 2012). Is she more eye candy than hero? Are any of the male characters portrayed in this way?

Consider if any female character has been "fridged." This term comes from the plot device known as "Women in Refrigerators," as named by comics writer Gail Simone (1999). It refers to Green Lantern Kyle Rayner opening his refrigerator to find his dead girlfriend in it, fueling a plot about his emotions over and actions because of her death. The larger point is that female characters are not infrequently made the targets of violence, especially sexualized violence, such that the plot of the story then explores that violence's effect on male characters and their development. The book that spurred Simone into beginning the list was *The Killing Joke*, in which Barbara Gordon/Batgirl is shot and paralyzed by the Joker. This story does not build her character in any way before that moment, nor does it explore the consequences of this life-changing traumatic event on her. Rather, the plot revolves around the Joker committing this crime to see how it will affect her father, Gotham Police Commissioner James Gordon, and Batman.

Another version of a female character being used to advance the development of the male characters is called the "Trinity Syndrome" after *The Matrix* movies. This is when a female character starts off as superior to or more powerful than a male character but then trains him up such that he surpasses her and becomes the protagonist and she is either sidelined or killed or both.[22] Like sexy lamps and fridgings, this narrative device employs women as objects rather than as fully fledged characters central to the plot of a story.

Conclusion

There is nothing "natural" or "normal" about the numerical inequities, different relationships to the plot, non-diverse and stereotypical portrayals, and objectification and sexualization of female characters versus male characters in superhero comics. Comics readers would do well to note the presence or absence of these types of representations,[23] enabling their recognition of the politics of gender in any given comic.

Works Cited

Bechdel, Alison. 1985. "The Rule." *Dykes to Watch Out For*: http://dykestowatchoutfor.com/the-rule.

Brown, Jeffrey. 2013. "Panthers and Vixens: Black Superheroines, Sexuality, and Stereotypes in Contemporary Comic Books." In *Black Comics: Politics of Race and Representation*, edited by Sheena Howard and Ronald Jackson II, 133-150. London: Bloomsbury, 2013.

Cocca, Carolyn. 2014a. "The Broke Back Test: A Quantitative and Qualitative Analysis of Portrayals of Women in Mainstream Superhero Comics, 1993-2013." *Journal of Graphic Novels and Comics* 5 (4): 411-428.

Cocca, Carolyn. 2014b. "Re-Booting Barbara Gordon: Oracle, Batgirl, and Feminist Disability Theories." *ImageText* 7 (4): http://www.english.ufl.edu/imagetext/archives/v7_4/cocca/.

---

[22] Robinson 2014.

[23] Helvie 2013 and Stuller 2012 have also both written to point readers toward several of the above elements in comics as well, applying them to Ms. Marvel and Lois Lane specifically.

Cocca, Carolyn. 2016. *Superwomen: Gender, Power, and Representation*. New York: Bloomsbury.

Helvie, Forrest. 2013 (November 21). "The Bechdel Test and a Sexy Lamp: Detecting Gender Bias and Stereotypes in Mainstream Comics." *Sequart*: sequart.org/magazine/34150/the-bechdel-test-and-a-sexy-lamp-detecting-gender-bias-and-stereotypes-in-mainstream-comics/.

Hudson, Laura. 2012 (March 19). "Kelly Sue DeConnick on the Evolution of Carol Danvers to Captain Marvel [Interview]." *Comics Alliance*: comicsalliance.com/kelly-sue-deconnick-captain-marvel/.

Prasso, Sheridan. 2005. *The Asian Mystique: Dragon Ladies, Geisha Girls, and Our Fantasies of the Exotic Orient*. New York: Public Affairs/Perseus Books.

Robinson, Tasha. 2014 (June 16). "We're Losing All Our Strong Female Characters to Trinity Syndrome." The Dissolve: thedissolve.com/features/exposition/618-were-losing-all-our-strong-female-characters-to-tr/.

Simone, Gail. 1999. "Women in Refrigerators:" lby3.com/wir/.

Stuller, Jennifer. 2012. "Second-wave Feminism in the Pages of *Lois Lane*." In *Critical Approaches to Comics. Theories and Methods*, edited by Matthew Smith and Randy Duncan, 235-251. New York: Routledge.

West, Carolyn. 2008. "Mammy, Jezebel, Sapphire, and Their Homegirls: Developing an 'Oppositional Gaze' Toward the Images of Black Women." In *Lectures on the Psychology of Women,* 4th ed., edited by Joan Chrisler, Carla Golden, and Patricia Rozee, 286-299. New York: McGraw Hill.

Queerness in Comics: How and Why to Review Comics Through the LGBTQIA+ Lens

by Michael Moccio

As hard as it is to communicate exactly what to look for when reviewing comics through an LGBTQIA+ lens, it's even harder to accomplish said task. So much analysis is based on perception, which can be clouded by unconscious bias: the bias that comics from living in a world that sends passive messages through media that perpetuate a culture that heavily favors heteronormativity, masculinity, ability, and cisgender individuals. We can only mitigate ourselves of our unconscious bias by understanding the communities portrayed in media as they are.

LGBTQIA+ stands for Lesbian, Gay, Bisexual, Trans, Queer, Intersex, and Asexual; the plus at the end designates the other sexualities, genders, and identities not included in those few letters. Some of these terms are comparatively newer – the acronym used to be simply LGBT, but has since grown to become more inclusive. While queer has a history of being a pejorative term against the gay community, some have since reclaimed it as an umbrella term for anyone who identifies as something other than heterosexual. Intersex is a term to describe those who naturally develop both male and female genitalia. Asexuality is a term to describe those who don't feel sexual attraction, not to be confused with celibacy. Other relevant terms to keep in mind include: cisgender, who are people whose gender aligns with their sex, and transphobia, the fear or hatred of trans individuals.[24]

While there is no "best way" to properly review LGBTQIA+ themes in comics, answering the following questions provide a good start:

1. Does this comic seek to tell a story about the lived experience of LGBTQIA+ individuals and what it's like to identify on the LGBTQIA+ spectrum, or are they simply including these characters for visibility?

---

[24] For more information on definitions related to the LGBTQIA+ community, the UC Davis LGBTQIA+ Resource Center Glossary has a good amount of definitions related to diversity and inclusion.

2. Does this comic perpetuate negative stereotypes and misconceptions about this marginalized community?

3. Are the characters and romances portrayed in this comic cisgender and heterosexual? If so, why?

Many writers and reviewers wouldn't think to ask these questions, often because they're not a part of the LGBTQIA+ community and don't immediately think of it. As a gay comics fan, it's always at the forefront of my mind.

With the explosion of comics catering towards more diverse audiences and as publishers' efforts to be more inclusive grows, it's important for all of us to understand how to effectively critique comments through the LGBTQIA+ lens.

It's too easy to brush off legitimate criticism and analysis as people trying to make comics "politically correct." If comics, despite a well thought out and executed storyline, misrepresented what it means to identify on the LGBTQIA+ spectrum and perpetuate negative stereotypes of the community, that can be extremely harmful to young LGBTQIA+ readers. It's our responsibility as reviewers to educate ourselves and hold not only the story's strength accountable, but also its impact.

While no one expects reviewers to research every facet of LGBTQIA+ life from the get go, it's important to research the relevant aspects when needed. For example, if you've never had to come out, how can you adequately determine whether a coming out scene feels "organic" without doing research? It's not enough to simply support marginalized groups like the LGBTQIA+ community. Reviewers must invest in research to understand the nuances of presentations of those identities when reviewing comics that try to tell a story about the lived experience of those in that community.

For LGBTQIA+ people, others denying your identity is dehumanizing. Whether it be sexual orientation or gender identity, it's no one's business but their own to say who they are and how they identify. So, when in *All New X-Men* #40, when Marvel Girl (Jean Grey) confronts Iceman (Bobby Drake) about his womanizing comments, she says point blank to him, "Bobby, you're gay."

For this example, Question #1 becomes important: with this interaction, writer Brian Michael Bendis doesn't only include LGBTQIA+ characters, he seeks to highlight their lived experiences: how Bobby chooses the identify and his own process with coming to terms with his sexuality. Despite this scene lasting two or three pages, it dominated conversation between reviewers, fans, and industry professionals alike. However, the focus was less on whether Marvel Girl decided Iceman's sexuality herself was problematic and more so on the continuity prior as evidence that Iceman simply couldn't be gay. Few tried to answer: what does it say that Marvel Girl psychically takes this information from Iceman's mind and then labels him instead of asking him without assumptions?

Where *All New X-Men* fumbled, Gail Simone's *Batgirl* succeeded. In *Batgirl* #19, Alysia Yeoh, admits in a moment of heartfelt emotion that she's trans, saying it was "something [she's] been trying to tell [Batgirl] for a while." Batgirl looks surprised for a moment and then reaffirms her unconditional love for Yeoh. The subtle difference between these two examples is that Simone clarifies Yeoh's gender identity to make the story more inclusive and diverse. At no point does the story explore what it means to be trans. Moreover, Yeoh's reaction is heartfelt and universal: the clear apprehension and utter relief conveyed through the artwork are emotions we've all endured when admitting something personal to those we care about. The focus remains squarely on the positive relationship between the characters and how this revelation doesn't make Yeoh any less or a woman or different from before.

In the two examples above, neither perpetuated negative stereotypes and misconceptions about the LGBTQIA+ community. Unfortunately, though, that does happen in comics.

In 2015, Image Comics launched a new series called *Airboy*, which followed fictionalized versions of writer James Robinson and artist Greg Hinkle as they try to find inspiration to write the adventures of the titular hero. Along the way, the character Airboy appears as a psychological projection only seen by Robinson and Hinkle. In the second issue, they go to a bar while under the influence of marijuana and Robinson has sex with a trans woman. Airboy has the same experience and becomes angry because he feels he's been "tricked."

This writing doesn't seek to explain the lived experiences of trans individuals, but playing into the negative stereotype of the deceitful trickster trope makes it transphobic. The interaction sends a message that engaging in sex with a trans individual is somehow lesser than sex with cisgender individuals.

Similarly, in 2014, DC Comics' *Batgirl* revitalized itself with a fresh new take on the character. In this storyline, Barbara Gordon is plagued by someone masquerading as Batgirl, ruining her reputation. As she goes on to solve the mystery, Batgirl finds out this mysterious individual is none other than artist Dagger Type, a man. When Batgirl unmasks Dagger Type in Batgirl #37, she exclaims in surprise, "But you're a –", and it's clear she meant to finish that sentence with "man."

Batgirl's expression is one of shock, almost disgust, when she finds Dagger underneath the cowl, playing into the harmful trope of the trans woman as the deceitful trickster. Moreover, Dagger makes a physical change once he's unmasked: his hair and eyes become wild, framed by his black mascara – he figuratively shapeshifts into a monster as his "true identity" is revealed. These kinds of stereotypes are believed as truths by people who harm trans individuals and members of the LGBTQIA+ community, and these portrayals reinforce these beliefs.

There are countless examples of how these lines of thinking cause deaths in the trans community. Trans women are murdered by men who use the gay panic defense, where they claim temporary insanity from the shock of the revelation. It wasn't until 2014 that California became the first state to ban trans panic and gay panic defenses in murder trials.

It's important to hold comics to a high standard if they support – inadvertently or otherwise – a reductive presentation of marginalized groups that reinforce misinformation and misperception about them, which others use as justifications when committing violence against trans individuals and members of the LGBTQIA+ community. Moreover, it's important for reviewers to hold themselves to high standards and not join in spreading misinformation.

Many reviewers and fans mislabeled Dagger Type as transgender, and they believed this to be fact because Type dressed as a woman. However, a more appropriate conclusion would be to say that he exhibits traits of a transvestite, which concerns wearing clothes ascribed to the opposite sex and usually has nothing to do with gender or sexual identity. Not many people outside of the LGBTQIA+ community can communicate the difference, simply because they don't know; reviewers must take on the onus of researching to properly analyze situations they may not have the knowledge of which to grasp the concept.

When members of the LGBTQIA+ community voiced their concerns over characters like Dagger Type, others defended the portrayal asking whether members of marginalized communities can ever be cast as villains? The reality is that we must examine the impact of these portrayals and determine whether they reinforce the reductive stereotypes and misperceptions about that marginalized groups. Similarly, it's not that writers can't present characters that hold stereotypes or bigoted views, but when the marginalized groups become the butt of the joke, reviewers must understand that communicates that those bigoted characters' views are correct.

The third question might seem arbitrary, but too often is the default character cisgender and heterosexual. Reviewers must be conscious of that and call to attention instances where comics stray from the norm, especially in a positive way.

One such series is *Lumberjanes*, a popular series published by BOOM! Studios, focused on a group of diverse, three-dimensional young girls that band together to confront the supernatural shenanigans going on at camp. Two campers, Molly and Mal, have a budding romance that's shown and threaded throughout the narrative – for an all ages title, it's huge that Lumberjanes can portray a healthy, normalized preteen relationship that sends positive messages to young, queer readers.

Additionally, Jo, the most level headed and analytical member of the group, comes out as trans in *Lumberjanes* #17 when she has a heart-to-heart with Barney of the Scouting Lads. Whereas the Lumberjanes are the equivalent to girl scouts, the Scouting Lads are the equivalent to boy scouts. The scene between those two characters was praised because there were substantial and organic scenes building up to it, making it clear this wasn't for shock value: previous issues showed childhood pictures of Jo presenting more masculine and she reacted aggressively as Barney began to realize maybe he would prefer being a Lumberjane rather than a Scouting Lad because it reminded her of her own transition.

Lumberjanes #28 continued Barney's character progression and culminates into one of the most memorable LGBTQIA+ scenes in mainstream comics. In this story arc, members of the High Council – the ruling authority of the Lumberjane Scouts – arrive at camp to check in; after being kidnapped, Barney helps rescue them. At the end, with help from Jo who has since turned into an ally and friend, Barney asks to join the Lumberjanes. The Council deliberates saying, "Highly unorthodox... Never allowed such a thing in our day... were there ever exceptions?"

The creative team plays on the expectation in that the Lodge would see Barney as a Scouting Lad and thus ineligible for the all-girls camp, which is why it's funny when they turn around and finish their thought, saying it's unorthodox "to allow admission to a camper mid-summer." Artists Ayme Sotuyo and Maarta Laiho can clearly express Barney's apprehension, surprise, and joy at the turn of events, making the scene that more visceral. The Council responds that the camp "is for hardcore lady-types. It's no one's place but yours to say whether you belong here." In a series of two panels, the entire creative team manage to evict a deep emotional response from the reader through a touching and powerful message that kids have the power to be themselves and aligns themselves with the identities to which they feel closest.

These narrative choices shape the message sent to readers. As reviewers, it's important to keep that in mind and evaluate whether these messages are positive or negative. Art doesn't exist in a vacuum: publishers and creative teams are responsible for the messages and themes they put out. As the industry evolves to cater to new audiences, reviewers must evolve accordingly to properly critique and analyze those stories.

That being said, reviewers also need to ensure they stay on topic and critique what's on the pages in the book. It's easy to stray and ask questions like, "What does it say when a cis creator writes about the experience of being trans instead of simply including a trans character in the narrative?" While questions like that are important and help hold the industry accountable for the creative teams they choose to tell their stories, that line of thought is best served in an editorial, not within the context of critiquing the actual comic book itself.

With that, there are plenty of online resources available, where LGBTQIA+ creators and professionals in the industry have spoken up about their experiences, where LGBTQIA+ individuals have shared their stories, and where you can expand your horizons to better understand the community and more effectively critiques comics that include aspects of said community. It's hard work, but ultimately worth it when we can all enjoy more positive diversity, representation, and inclusion in the medium.

Addressing and Improving Toxic Masculinity in Comics Through Better Reviews

by Ryan K. Lindsay

Toxic Masculinity is a very large issue residing within the core of comics culture and there is absolutely zero reason to accept this as a truth we can't affect. From 'old boy' gatekeepers, sweaty underground dungeons full of back issues and judgemental glares, and the harassment that permeates the back channels of conventions, editorial offices, and online social media, to the story choices that overtly and subliminally marginalise anyone not white and male, and that also reinforce the concept of emotionless violence as a solution, comics have a lot of improvement to make and everyone can play a small part in a big movement.

Many see comics as a medium for men, and a specific kind of man, and while it's not true – comic readers are diverse and beautiful and intelligent in all kinds of ways – it would be remiss to not try and address the fact that hypermasculinity and dudebro culture can be rife in comics on and behind the page and that reviewers can and should play a great part in fighting against this to make comics a universally communal and safe space to enjoy.

The first *major* lesson in writing about toxic masculinity in comic works is to call out that rubbish for what it is because it harms the medium, as well as the people who love it.

Silence is a *strong factor* as to why this garbage permeates. A clear voice, backed up by reason, calmly and firmly putting things out there can do a lot of good in this world. The very simple dictum to live by is: if you see something, say something.

Acting against harassment and toxic environments is always the best engagement to end these things, and just talking about them openly, making them a part of regular discourse, can have a hugely positive effect in pushing change. If you have a large following who trust your words then you can open them up to positive influences and new angles from which to consider things. This level of influence can never be discounted in the ongoing desire to improve anything – words do have power.

On the page, there are the alpha male leading characters that clog the shelves, the heroes saving the princesses, the sad string of tired sexist cliches. There's also a stereotypical square jaw given to every male lead who feels no pain, inside or out, and handles his problems with his fists drawing them closer to punch them while also forever pushing these problems away.

There are many familiar tropes that are no longer needed in stories and nor should we allow others to get lazy and rely upon them. The Bechdel Test is easy to pass, there need not be women in refrigerators anymore, and the Sexy Lamp test is just sad that it needs to exist, no less have people failing it.[25]

So, what to do when you want to comment about something that's slid in as subpar and it's bolstering up a cliche culture of comics being driven by a rotten core of masculine agendas that don't understand nor value women and use them as either plot tokens or else something to be ogled, handled, and discarded?

When writing about these aspects of comics consider these two tactics. Tackle the problem head on, in context, and do it firmly and clearly. Then, consider raising the bar by offering a comparison study.

An example might be looking at something as wholeheartedly ridiculous as the Manara Spider-Woman cover in your article/review. The decision for Marvel to hire Milo Manara – a renowned Italian artist whose depictions of females and sexuality is well crafted, but ill-suited to mainstream Marvel work due to its graphic nature and overt hypersexuality – to illustrate an overly-sexed variant cover for Spider-Woman as she climbs sensuously onto a rooftop with an exaggerated and anatomically awkward bow to accentuate her curves was inherently thoughtless from the start. To get this point across, you are allowed to acknowledge the fact that Manara's art is beautiful and it does what it aims to do very well. But alongside craft you should also consider the context of placement of this art. A book about an empowered female superhero is not the place to play this hypersexualised image because it acts against the core of the book, and is so far against the readership of the book that it's counterproductive and may drive them away.

---

[25] For further discussion of the Bechdel Test and the Sexy Lamp Test, see "The Bechdel Test and a Sexy Lamp: Detecting Gender Bias and Stereotypes in Mainstream Comics." *Sequart Organization*, Sequart, 21 Nov 2013.

This is the context of the problem and is an effective way for you to address the argument. The exact same thing can be said about the Rafael Albuquerque cover for *Batgirl* that was an homage to *The Killing Joke*, wherein the Joker stands behind her, dressed in his iconic purple garb from the Brian Bolland/Alan Moore classic, and holds a finger like a gun to her head while a frightened expression reads across her face and a tear wells in her terrified eye. Yes, that was beautiful art, you are allowed to appreciate how fantastic Albuquerque's style is, but you have to put forward the proposition that the context of that cover – showing a female superhero in a situation that's drawing from the continuity of the time she was sexually assaulted and crippled, and doing this on the front of the new title where it's consciously aimed at bringing in young female readers and giving them a safe place to explore a fan-favourite character without fear of refrigerators or sexy lamps actually applying – means that the cover didn't fit, it was harmful, and was deserving of its negative reception.

And you can do this with any piece of art that isn't passing muster – a storyline, a character, a panel. If you see something, then talk about it. Raise the issue openly, not as something you are necessarily attacking – and it's not always personally, and rarely should be – but as something you want to discuss and dissect.

Allow yourself to look past the quality of the work sometimes and place it into context. This is just as important an indicator of art's success and validity as whether the lines and colors work. Because it's easy to sit back and enjoy nice art, but it's harder [and yet still often so important] to consider the implications, even subtly, of that art and what it might mean to people other than yourself. It is to ask art whether it is helping or not. It's a hard thing to do, it requires you to consider other aspects and angles, but once you start doing it then you'll find your eyes are far more open to the concept of how art works rather than accepting it for the way it has always worked.

The majority of comics are made by straight white men, and it feels like this is reflected in much of the cultural critique of these works. This could speak to why archaic ideas and manners still systemically proliferate despite the fact the medium is neither for nor actually completely by straight white men.

Anytime toxic masculinity is pressing down – killing female characters to drive the male protagonist's plot forward, making fun of sexual orientations considered outside the norm in subtle and insidious ways [which is often done simply by presenting anyone outside of the straight white formula as the 'other' and having them be foreign and different], or not even writing any female characters or those of diverse ethnicities or sexual orientations – you need to see these problems and omissions and then you can call them out.

There will be times when the comic isn't problematically ignoring the inclusion of other people outside the straight white guy paradigm, but you are still allowed to call this out. You can and should start to see that a story with only straight white guys in it is a poor understanding of what humanity is like in the 21st century. In this instance, you might not want to feel like you are 'calling out' anything negative and so there is another handy tactic to take.

There are also the times where an all-male comic has the propensity to be masculine, and to push masculinity in ways in which it doesn't need promotion. Hyper-violent resolutions to problems where no one is talking enough. The idea that might makes right and that those showing weakness will be relegated to the back of the pack, or just simply murdered or excommunicated.

This kind of concept, played out regularly in stories everywhere, is harmful to growing minds, and also helps build a society where men's mental health issues continue to be ignored because men don't talk about their feelings. And it's not completely asinine to wonder why all male superheroes only ever sort out their problems with their fists and never seem to feel any consequences from their actions otherwise. There is merit in calling this kind of thing out, do so by questioning the work, pondering aloud the current relevancy of what it is doing. You can also point to where it gets done well, because if you're going to point out a problem then you might as well offer a solution. Lead the discussion forward and give positive examples to reinforce your point.

Raise the subject of Tony Stark's PTSD in the *Iron Man 3* film as an example of how superhero comics can begin to portray realistic masculinity in non-harmful shades of stereotypes. This brings about the topic that violence has real world considerations to be taken into account and that men can be fallible.

Goran Parlov and Garth Ennis made *Fury Max: My War Gone By*, which was a maxi series that could not be more masculine in the way it depicts war and spies and violence and sex. But at the core of that project, the book was about the fact that being that man, living that powerful life of being an object in the world comprised of all edges and no soft spots, and never wavering from the path was only going to have one consequence means you will end up a shell of a man. You will miss out on someone who could be the love of your life, you will have forged no real connections in this world based on anything beyond the bond of battles, or the clash of rivalry and begrudging contempt. You will have filled out the complete guide on 'How to be a Manly Man' but in the end you'll barely be a man because you'll have and feel nothing.

Parlov / Ennis created a book that perfectly defines why and how toxic masculinity works and remains. When you critique this book, before the Dave Johnson covers get a mention, before you dive into the historical authenticity of the planes and location, before you marvel at how unwaveringly heroic and stony Nick Fury is, take a moment to launch your thoughts about the book and the themes represented that matter. Don't save the juicy stuff for the second last paragraph, don't hide it away, don't tap away at your keyboard crafting a synopsis, no, start smashing the theme and see what comes out. This kind of analysis is the important part of the book and you need not hide it away. It'll illuminate the text as well as have the chance to expand minds who might then check out the book or who did not consider this angle from their first reading of the text.

Discuss the meaty themes that will get people to consider the implications of these texts, and if you find them lacking then point to the ones that get it right and / or lament the fact that real world aspects are missing and would be beneficial to include in future works.

There is merit to be had in taking texts that we normally see and label as "normal" and digging into them a little to scrape away the systemic sexism and racism that we barely notice through a filter of pop culture that promotes and floods us with these things that are no good for us and certainly no longer good enough for any of us. Step back, analyse to see if you have considered context or aspects of toxic masculinity at play, and then say something in productive ways. You will be alarmed at how many examples you will quickly find all around you, but you will very quickly be pleased by how much more you have to say about them each time.

Deep-Dive Creator Interviews

As mentioned before, students, journalists, and critics of all backgrounds can learn a great deal by understanding the process behind creating comics from the perspective of those who create them. In our Deep-Dive interviews, I spoke with editors, writers, and artists – many of whom come from a teaching background – to explore their understanding of the role of the critic in relation to the creator as well as ways to better understand the craft of creating comics so that critics and those writing about comics can further understand the medium as a whole.

Although readers may notice that many of the questions I posed the different creators are the same or similar, it's worth pointing out both the differences and similarities in their responses. The similarities may be seen to reflect a shared awareness amongst professionals within the comics community, and yet, those differences that come to light often result from each person's unique perspective on the business of creating comics and the medium as a whole. As a result, readers can gain that much more appreciation and understanding of these expressions of creative art and storytelling all the more.

Brian Michael Bendis (*Action Comics*, *Ultimate Spider-Man*, Jinx World)

Forrest C. Helvie: As someone who works with students in either creative writing or art classes, how often do you have students engage in peer review? What are some of the guidelines you put in place to help your students provide their peers with useful feedback and constructive criticism?

Brian Michael Bendis: First and foremost, think about what they're pitching — not what you think or wish they were pitching. Think about what they want to write and not what you want to write. Be honest with the writer. In the class at Portland State University where I teach a comic writing class, there was this one semester where almost everyone in the class wanted to write about magical dragon eggs — no idea why! But they were into them to such a point where I thought they were joking around with me. It was a great opportunity for me, as I don't care about those kinds of stories, but as a critic, that doesn't matter. Does the story make sense? Is it the best version of that story that could be told? That's what matters in criticism.

Learn that you cannot make everyone happy, and stop trying. It cannot be done. Someone doesn't like Star Wars. Someone doesn't like The Beatles. And knowing this can be freeing as a creative person.

Helvie: What are the top mistakes that you can think of that critics make when reviewing or analyzing comics?

Bendis: I was a huge fan of Siskel and Ebert — pre-internet. It was this wonderful, one-stop-shop place to go to get informed reviews and critiques of pop culture products, namely film, where they would often bitch at one another. I recall this one review where they were reviewing each other. They were both very on the spot, but it was for *Home Alone* and Siskel said something to the effect of "I wish they would have made a movie about what it really felt like to be home alone. The feel, the panic ... really get into it." But then Ebert said "Yeah, but they didn't even try that. Why are you judging them on something they didn't even attempt?" Then they started arguing about what their roles really were, and I think it was a really valuable moment about the state of criticism.

I've since pointed that out as my number one example of where we see critics say "You know what they should have done..." When you do that, you are no longer analyzing and reviewing; instead, you're writing. You're looking to add or subtract from the narrative presented. As a reviewer, you need to ask yourself when doing that, do you want to review or write? Some of the best writers started as critics, and that's fine. But you need to make a choice about what game you want to play. Don't let your subconscious creep out from your critique and begin attempting to write the story you wanted to write.

Helvie: Is there a place for the critic to suggest to the writer for what could have / should have been done?

Bendis: Not really. Not if the person is trying to be a critic. And there are some who clearly wanted to be comic writers rather than comic critics. And I don't mean this in a cruel or condescending way. I don't! Go be a comic writer! It's fun! It's much better than spewing forth rage about something you love! I have found that most critiques come from a place of love. If you're spending time writing about a comic, you get how personal it is, and you want to share it with others. Just make sure you do it with all the tools and knowledge available to you.

Helvie: Is there a particular characteristic that either turns you on or off in a critique?

Bendis: Sometimes, it's just about the approach. Whenever I see someone who approaches a review with "For all of Stephen King's past work..." or "With all of Neil Gaiman's experience..." I wonder if I'm dealing with a jealous critic. And they're going to do their part to take the writer down a peg or two. Of course, I can't say for sure that's what's going on, but maybe there's something at a subconscious level that needs to be looked into, you know? Some people own it, but there are some people who are not in touch with their flaws, and they should as it will creep out into their writing.

But when I see a heartfelt, passionate disagreement? I'll respect that. When you look at *Civil War 2*, there are two groups of heroes who are fighting over an idea and there's no hard-and-fast right or wrong. And I knew people were going to be divided on what I was doing there. It was built for people to fight over. Some people recognized what we were doing and criticized the work for what it was; others, however, took it quite personally and became personal in their criticism. A professional critique can have a voice, but it needs to be professional. Respectful even in the face of dislike.

Here's a good rule of thumb: How often did you write the word "I" in your review or critique? Who is taking the spotlight in the analysis and who or what should be the subject?

Helvie: What do you think are the 2-3 most important elements that critics need to look for in a story? When you are sitting at home putting the narrative together, what should they focus on more than anything else?

Bendis: Intention. If you can't tell, that's a problem. You're involved in a story that's supposed to move you. I remember one critique where the writer claimed I "manipulated" them into feeling a certain way as if that was a flaw, but the goal for me was to affect them in that way. Going back to the Siskel and Ebert argument, it comes down to what was the team intending? If you as the critic can't tell, then that's probably a bad sign. But if you are moved by something that didn't spell itself out for you, you're involved in a great experience regardless of whether it was one you were looking for or not. A good horror story will terrify you whether you like that feeling or not. One might say that the best horror stories are those that you hate the most if you don't like being scared! But if your job is to critique that? It's your job to recognize the skill displayed in the telling of that story.

Helvie: Brian, you mention professionalism in criticism. Can you share a thought or two about what you think the difference is between professional criticism and perhaps, amateur criticism?

Bendis: I am really trepiditious about using the word "amateur." You don't necessarily need to go to school to be trained in criticism, although you certainly can, but you do need to at least train yourself. Learn about your field. I often see critics making the very mistakes that they're critiquing someone else for.

Helvie: Is there anything else you would suggest for critics seeking to publish their work that they ought to consider?

Bendis: The second point I would bring up is, and I understand this is a generality, I think many critics can be thin-skinned. Why would you be so harsh to a creative team if you can't handle the feedback? Maybe be more willing take on more responsibility for what you say. I don't want to dive into why that is or where that insecurity comes from, but it's something to think about. And I get it: Putting yourself out there is tough and having a lot of people read what you write is not always going to be well-received. But it's something to keep in mind.

Take yourself seriously. It sounds simple, but I do see a lot of writers excuse themselves when they get called out for publishing a poorly written review by saying "I didn't get paid for it. What can you expect?" I understand, believe me, I do. It's tough making a break out there. But if you want people to take you seriously as a writer, you need to stand behind your work, paid or not, as that speaks volumes about your professionalism. It's something I've certainly seen make or break professional and up-and-coming critics.

Helvie: Can you tell me about the harshest – but more fairly written – review you received? What made it fair and why did you give it credence?

Bendis: It's a good question and it happens often! There isn't just one. Half of those would be published reviews, but some are even as simple fan interactions through social media. I look at that tweet and say to myself "Yeah, you know? I think you may be right." I'm a little older now and have better perspective. I'm trying to write a truth, you know? Whose truth is more true? If they match, then they like me. If they don't, then they'll call me out. But here's something that keeps me anchored: No matter what a critic says, if I loved a work and everyone hates it, I'm still going to love it. And if, in my heart, I know it wasn't done well, no critic will convince me that it was or wasn't good.

But if I've been called on something that's objectively a fact? Well, a fact's a fact and to get that wrong simply means you need take that hit on the chin.

Helvie: Given the rise in prominence of social media over the past two decades, we have even more venues for interaction between the creator and critic. Is there a place for the two sides to interact with one another?

Bendis: I think the interactions between the creator and critic should be minimal. In reading Warren Beatty's autobiography, it talks about how he bought the critic Pauline Kael and put her to work! It was crazy to read! There should be a line of fire – a friendly one – but we want to keep things pure. I know I'm probably alone in that, but I should create what I create and the critic should create what they create. They should keep an open mind and heart, of course, but the distance needs to be kept. You put your work out for critique and critiques will come.

Even at a young age, I remember not taking criticism well and needing time to process. Your first reaction may not be your best reaction, so creators need to give themselves the time to process things and see if there might have been some truth to it. And I imagine the same goes for critics and their writing as well. Of course, everyone wants to publish something and see the reading audience say "Yay!" but that's not going to happen often. And that's a big disappointment.

Helvie: Do you find yourself critiquing others as a fellow creator?

Bendis: I've learned to curb my critiques of myself and others out of respect for my collaborators and my fans. I've seen those director's cut films where the team is shitting all over a film to such an extent that I can no longer even enjoy it. I don't want to do that to someone else! There's a point where you have to say "This isn't fun for anybody!"

Helvie: So, in a way, it seems like you're suggesting that creators need to remove themselves from the critiquing process?

Bendis: Yes. If I hear something that rings true, then it will be applied immediately. It's going to stay and inform what I do from that point onward. But otherwise, I want to keep out of engaging with critics about the criticism.

Helvie: Now, you're framing that from the perspective of a creative person, but do you think that applies to the critic?

Bendis: Absolutely! Don't write for the creators or publishers. If you write honestly for yourself, people will come to it. It's one of the biggest lessons to learn for writers of any type, and it's one I try to make sure my students get early on. Sometimes it can take decades for people to finally get it. I've seen people ruin careers chasing the crowds.

Helvie: Shifting gears a bit, comics are a collaborative medium – not just between the writer and artist/s but also the editor. Are there times when you've had your work critiqued – positively or negatively – and it was actually something someone else from your team did? How should critics handle this? We're in a period with comics where there is a real need to credit all members of the team, but what do you think is a viable means of doing this when unsure of each member's exact contributions?

Bendis: It *is* a tough thing to do. I see this as much in film criticism as I do in comics criticism. When I see a film critic who really knows their stuff, they know what a cinematographer does and it shows in their review. On the other hand, I've seen other nationally-known critics make it clear they really don't know who does what or who's responsible for what or why something makes the audience feel a certain way.

The critic who wants to be taken seriously needs to do their homework and know their stuff. If you're going to take the time to write something about a comic – either it moves you positively or negatively to take the time out to write about it – you should do it the courtesy of knowing what you're writing about. You can't know every secret fact about a particular comic's creation, but you can know the roles that go into making comics, who generally does what, and tread humbly from there. And look, mistakes will be made, and that happens, but it generally shouldn't be born out of a lack of awareness of creative responsibilities on the part of the critic. I've even looked at movies and wondered why the writer came up with some dialogue, but then I realized the actor or director may have gone in after the fact and added that. You just can't know all things with 100% certainty.

And I try to curtail my critiques of others' comics because it could be the fault of the people you know, but it could also be the fault of someone else. Panels and dialogue could be edited post-production and the credited team would be left on the line.

Helvie: How much should the critic hold the creative team accountable to the format? For example, if we look at the monthly floppy issue, does each issue need to be 100% accessible to new readers? Perhaps more in tune with the superhero genre, how much background familiarity with continuity and characters should readers have?

Bendis: Regardless of format, the comic needs to provide an entertaining experience. When I've read comics where I hadn't had access to the first two or three chapters, and I still didn't feel cheated, it made me feel like "Ooohh! I need to go get those back issues!" That's a very different response than "Oh. I guess I need to go get those back issues." I think about this all of the time. Creators have to tell a story that will work for both returning and newly arrived reading audiences.

Now that said, if you know going into writing a critique or analysis where you don't like a particular format (e.g. monthly issues, graphic novels, etc.), that's not really a fault to put on the work. Instead, the critic might better aid his or her readers in suggesting what did work within those parameters. But other than that, I don't see how it helps anyone as people reading your review are probably a fan of that given format.

Helvie: Ultimately, what value do you find in criticism? There are a lot of people today who like to claim the critics are useless. Is this fair?

Bendis: This is something Matt Fraction and I share a deep fondness for — pulling something apart and seeing what it was made. When I teach my students, I rely on them to be able to do the same. I will put a piece of famous comic art on the board and ask them to write the script as they see it. Deep, critical analysis of published work is a big part of learning the craft. I don't know how you could do it without.

Helvie: We live in the age of the internet where everyone can put their two cents out there. Do you think this has affected criticism positively or negatively?

Bendis: People are feeling the authority of the critic slipping away almost completely. Everyone's opinion is equal. But I've seen some professional critics really up their game and show their readers why it is they should come and read their reviews. They're going to offer a particular voice, perspective and flavor that can't be found elsewhere. And I've seen other critics really struggle to find that voice. It's interesting how the critic has to perform to be heard now unlike before.

Comfort Love and Adam Withers (*The Uniques, Rainbow in the Dark*)

Forrest C. Helvie: Overall, what do you think are the three most important skills or elements a critic needs to be aware of when reviewing a comic?

Comfort Love and Adam Withers: We think there are three major things a critic needs in order to deliver useful, helpful review – both in terms of helping an audience understand and appreciate a work, and in terms of the professional being able to draw something of value from the critique.

First, you have to know the difference between objective and subjective criticism. There are objective aspects to art and writing, especially in comics where the goal is to communicate a story to an audience. You can write your story in a way that is objectively difficult to understand, or use plot points and narrative or character beats that are objectively stale and overused, redundant or poorly set up. The same is true for the art – an artist can fail or succeed on objective grounds, creating art that fails to communicate what is needed to the audience, or which excels in certain fundamental ways.

Then there's the subjective side, which is personal taste. What we like, what we don't; the things that have nothing to do with what the creators have done, but with our interpretation of it and how our preferences and history impact that interpretation. No critic can *or should* avoid subjective review. Most times when creators or readers get angry about a critic's work, it's because that person's subjective experience didn't match the reader's, and therefore they *must be wrong!!!* But writing about subjective and objective experience is crucial to understanding both what a work is doing and the impact it's having, both good and bad.

Therefore, a critic has to be able to balance objective review with subjective observation, and to keep that somewhat clear for the audience. You can like something that's objectively bad, and dislike something objectively well-made. A perfect example is *Watchmen.* By every objective measure, it is a brilliant work. It uses the artform of comics to tell a story that maximizes all the best parts of the medium, doing something only comics can do and showcasing everything they can be. But, while unquestionably an objective masterpiece, that doesn't mean everybody is going to enjoy it on a subjective level. It's a difficult balance to maintain, but a necessary one.

Helvie: You mention the need to balance objective review with subjective observation. How can one do that effectively?

Love and Withers: This brings us to the second major tool a critic needs: a deep understanding of their own biases. All too often we see collections of "Top 10 _____" where every entry feels like another version of the same piece of work. A list of the best covers of the year where they all look more or less the same, or a list of the best ongoing series that focuses on one or two genres, one or two story types. That's a lack of recognition of bias. The critic has a "type" they gravitate toward, and mistakenly presume that the kind of thing they like best is the best kind of thing to like. As we said, reporting on subjective experience is *important!* How a work impacted you on a personal level matters, and we've frequently been moved to try a story because of how a critic described their experience with it. The only way to recognize the difference between objective and subjective criticism is to know yourself, know your preferences, and try to recognize when your blinders are on.

Helvie: Alright. So, we're aware of the need for both objectivity and subjectivity in our analysis in addition to being more aware of our biases. What's the most effective means to ensure we communicate our thoughts without crossing those lines?

Love and Withers: This brings us to our final point: A critic needs to have a handle on language. A review is no good to anyone if it becomes too broad, too vague – only through specificity can meaning be understood! In other words, if something isn't working, why isn't it? What is the specific problem, and how can you best describe that failure? Don't just say the art is good or bad, but explain *why!* And your vocabulary has to be accessible; don't get caught up using industry lingo or complicated terminology, write in a way that both expert and layman can easily understand. A review isn't an opportunity for you to look smarter than the creator, it's for the benefit of your readers – a critique that's so overly-intellectualized as to become a grandiloquent word salad is a pretentious failure. So broad "I don't know, it just wasn't working" kind of statements aren't helpful or informative, but explaining yourself with terminology your readers won't understand isn't helpful either.

Helvie: You are both educators in addition to being artists. How do you teach your art students to review one another's work?

Love and Withers: When working with our students, we have every major project culminate in a full-class critique, but the project isn't actually collected and graded until they've had a week after that critique to make any changes they want to. What's the point of that kind of review if you can't actually do anything with the feedback you're given? This allows them to immediately put theory into practice and grow as artists. To the extent that they express their critique through suggesting alternative solutions, it's often hard for young creators to know how to think critically without slipping into a kind of problem solving mentality. And that's okay, given the context – a classroom critique is not just a forum to judge something's quality for the sake of some other audience listening in, but for a group of artists to help each other improve. The worst it can do is present a possible solution that doesn't fit the artist's vision or style, but they'll still walk away knowing something isn't working in their piece and they'll need to figure out their own solution to the problem.

Helvie: Do you think writers can review and analyze comics in the same way?

Love and Withers: While that works well for artists in an open critique session, it isn't a very good way to approach criticism. That's a different forum with a different audience and different goals. It isn't the critic's job to tell the creators how to improve; they're there to help an audience understand the quality of a work and if it's worth their time.

Helvie: So making suggestions for how to tell the story need to be left out altogether then?

Love and Withers: If a critic wants to suggest alternatives for a story, use a different forum for that – maybe some kind of "Reimagining Stories" column where you have different stories and give alternate takes on how you'd write them. But that isn't effective as criticism. We've had people offer critiques of our comics that wound up being lists of "Make it about this character instead," or "Change your art style so it looks more like this other artist I like better." That isn't helpful for us, because that isn't the story we're trying to make or the style we want to draw it in. And it isn't helpful for the audience, because they don't necessarily care what kind of story you'd rather be reading. They want to know what this particular book is about and how well it's executed. Giving them some theoretical fantasy book you'd like better doesn't serve that purpose.

Helvie: One of the difficulties in critiquing comics – unlike a traditional prose text – is that there are multiple players contributing to the creation of that story, from the writer and artist to the colorist, letterer, and even editor. How does someone make the call, in terms of attributing credit to the different creators? Or should they not worry about figuring out who contributed what elements?

Love and Withers: If a penciller and inker are working together, never speak of their work individually. You never know how much the inker is bringing to the table, and so must always assume it's an equal share. Some of the most renowned artists of our time had work that would be unrecognizable without their inking partners. That role deserves respect, so write about the artists as a team rather than an individual.

Helvie: Okay, so we should primarily try to assess the work – artistically – from the perspective of seeing it as a "team" effort – though still separate from the writing?

Love and Withers: A critic judges the quality of a final product, and its creation plays a part in the background of that product but doesn't automatically change the result. It isn't a critic's job to micromanage which part of a team is responsible for which part of a story, other than judging the art distinctly (but not entirely separately) from the writing. If something in your comic isn't working, it's on you as the creator. It doesn't matter if your editor made you do it, or if some outside factor forced a change – the only thing that matters is the final product and the name in the credits. It's an unfortunate truth, but still true; the solution is to learn the kind of confidence and inoffensive assertiveness that will help you better take the reins of your own story. It isn't the responsibility of the critic to cut you extra slack because that story beat "wasn't your fault," any more than it's the responsibility of the reader to research a comic's editor to see if they have a history of meddling with stories or whatever.

The only thing that should matter to the critic is that the story is well-told and impactful; in other words, it should make sense, follow a logical sequence of events, and make you feel something as you read it. If a lack of accessibility to the story hurts the reading experience, that's a problem worth criticizing. If the story works well regardless, then accessibility obviously wasn't a hurdle. You shouldn't have to know the "rules" of a comic's genre to enjoy the story – does the book work, or not? Did you feel something while you read it? Was it engaging? Then it worked. If you can't appreciate a work without first understanding some deeper history of its genre, it isn't a very good piece of work.

Helvie: So, if a critic doesn't necessarily need to know the "rules" of the comics genre, are there any basic elements should they know?

Love and Withers: There does need to be recognition of the different roles in comics. Don't say the writer didn't do his job if it's the artist making things confusing to read. Don't blame the artist that the letterer crowded the bubbles with too much text (that might even have been the writer's fault!). A good critic is knowledgeable enough about the various roles in making a comic to be able to tell when a mistake was bad lettering, bad writing, or bad art, and can explain precisely *why* it isn't working.

Helvie: Okay, so there are some basic building blocks in relation to comics that critics should have. Most writers know the rules of narrative but when it comes to art, that depth of knowledge tends not to be as deep. Where does one begin?

Love and Withers: A critic needs to know enough about art to be able to point out specific strengths and weaknesses of an artist. As we said before, vague criticism is unhelpful criticism. Never settle for saying something "just feels *off* somehow..." Figure out *why* it feels off to you and write *that.* You don't have to be a capable artist to comment on art, any more than you need to make movies to be able to be a good film critic. You just need to know enough to speak from a place of knowledge rather than making broad, sweeping statements that wind up saying nothing of substance.

Helvie: I know you both published *The Complete Guide to Self-Publishing Comics,* which covers a lot of this ground. Are there any other texts you would recommend to help introduce critics and reviewers to learning more about comic art?

Love and Withers: Probably the most important thing to understand about the art of comics is the way it contributes to storytelling. *Understanding Comics* makes this easy for the non-artist to grasp, but there are elements to comics art that move beyond illustration and into a kind of visual writing. What J.R.R. Tolkien would say about a rolling hill and patch of wood might take several pages; the comics artist shows you in one panel, while losing none of the richness of detail from the author. The comics artist is single-handedly filling the role of director and cinematographer, sets all the lighting, dresses all the sets, and is every actor in the production. No film critic would ignore the storytelling value of these people, so don't look at a comics artist as simply illustrating the writer's words. They bring the words to life, give them movement, give them emotion we can see on the page rather than just in our minds, and set the pace and tone of the story through the kinds of visuals they choose.

Helvie: As we bring things to a close, let's look at the role and the value that you see critics and reviewers of all backgrounds bringing to the greater comics medium.

Love and Withers: As creators, our highest priority has to be doing what's best for the story. That means if readers and critics say something isn't working, we have to listen. It doesn't mean we have to *agree*, and that's a crucial distinction, but we have to be open to the possibility that we're messing something up without realizing it. You can be so close to a work you're creating that you don't notice problems right under your nose. Good criticism can point things out to you that you'd never noticed. It can show you different interpretations of your words and art that you hadn't anticipated. If the goal of a great comic is to communicate in both ideas and emotion with its audience (and that should always be the goal), then the creator is only half the conversation. The audience is the other half, and their interpretation matters. Communication is about both intention and impact – we can control our intention, but we have to be aware of our impact. If they aren't lining up, if we're trying to say one thing but another is being received, then we have to change our approach to bring intention and impact into better alignment.

Helvie: Are there dangers to paying too much attention to the critics?

Love and Withers: Sometimes the critics are wrong. Sometimes the readers missed something, or don't have the whole story yet. Often, your ideas about a story at issue five are very different from when you've reached issue 20. Creators have to balance our desire to have people picking up what we're doing every issue with our need to stay focused on the long game. We have to recognize when a certain amount of miscommunication is actually okay in the pursuit of the longer-term story. Eventually all will be clear, we can hope. Eventually, they'll see where we were going and appreciate the journey. But there's nothing wrong with a little course-correction along the way, if we have to, to make that journey as rewarding for everyone as it can be.

Jim Zub (*Uncanny Avengers, Wayward, Skullkickers*)

Forrest C. Helvie: Let's start with taking a look at comics press – the reviewers in particular. How many do you find actually know how to engage in the craft of writing reviews well?

Jim Zub: It's partially this idea of what you like and don't like. Then there is this formal codification of discussing why you like or do not like something. You can and should go into depth about this. But I want to be careful about not getting into the business of critiquing criticism. It's like a snake eating its own tail.

Helvie: Understood. And we certainly aren't looking to have you engage in telling the critic how to do his or her job. But do you think there is some benefit for critics to engage with the creators as a way to hone their respective craft?

Zub: If any creator tells you they don't read reviews, they're lying. Any creator who says they ignore the reviews, they're lying. If they tell you that good reviews don't make them feel good, they're also lying. It's just that some people are better than others at lying about the same thing. Everyone wants the compliments, but everyone wants to steer away from the criticism.

I get it. The only time I'll engage in the criticism, however, is when there is a factual error in what the reviewer says, like a miscredit or something patently untrue. Not opinion but something they're simply incorrect or misinformed about. Otherwise, I try to steer clear of engaging in the criticism.

Helvie: What was the harshest but the most fairly written critique you've received?

Zub: There were people who, when we were starting with *Wayward*, they mentioned the plot was racing forward too quickly and not allowing readers to get to know the characters in great enough depth. And you know? I had been feeling that way, too, in spots. In creator-owned books, you don't have the same editorial feedback as you do in work-for-hire. If you're not careful, you can get lost in the weeds.

Helvie: So, it's possible for critics to provide some value to the creative community. How difficult was it to hear?

Zub: Mind you, some of these critics didn't relay that message kindly! They were harsh on the book, and I thought "Ouch! Take it easy!" There was still another reviewer who never seemed to like the book but they kept reviewing each and every issue. I couldn't help but wonder why they were continuing to hold on to this thing they were clearly not enjoying. That felt punishing. Why were they doing this not only to me but also themselves? Clearly, it wasn't written for them, and even when they complimented it on occasion, it was this odd and begrudging sort of moment.

Helvie: In a sense, there's a balance then between delivering a critical message but perhaps doing it in such a fashion that is less personal and more professional then?

Zub: Exactly. I think we sometimes see in critics that there's a binary approach to a comic. It's either good or it's crap. You know, there's no job on earth where you can tell people what they're doing is crap and they're going to continue hiring you. Your priority list might not be the same as mine, and it's important to recognize that.

Helvie: I'm going to shift gears a bit here, but there's another phenomenon that earns a good many comics press folk a bad name and that is using their current platform of writing about comics as a stepping stone to creating comics. Have you seen much of this?

Zub: There's no nice way to put this, so I'll just lay it out there: There's a disproportionate number of reviewers who are would-be comic book writers. They view it through the lens of "I want to be your friend" or "I want to tell you how to do things differently because I want your job." See, that's another form of weird sort of egocentric interactions that takes place all too frequently. And I'm not sure where to go with that. It's a real Pandora's Box.

Helvie: This is always interesting to me as it pertains to comics because in traditional literature, there are many writers who both create fictional stories but also engage in critical discourse.

Zub: What do you think of that?

Helvie: Admittedly, I'm biased as I'm someone who does that! In truth, though, I think there's real value in deeply exploring both sides. As a comics critic, I've learned so much more about the process by engaging in it firsthand. Likewise, I've become a better storyteller through being aware of the technical aspects that I'm looking for as a critic. But it's essential to avoid those conflicts of interest and prevent your lines from crossing.

Zub: Comics, as big as they are and can be, they still feel like a weird, scrappy community. So don't shit where you eat. Of course, I consume many comics and I'm highly critical of what I read. My wife and I sit and read before we go to bed, and we go through it extensively. It helps me learn and grow. But that's for my own personal understanding. It's not me going on a soapbox and telling them who is right and who is wrong. It's a personal sort of thing. Creators whom I'm friends with and respect, we talk.

Helvie: So, you're saying that a greater context is important for the critic to keep in mind?

Zub: When I was student and thought I knew everything once I'd gathered a little bit of knowledge, I would say "This person is crap. What an embarrassment." Then you go and become a professional, and you learn even more. Those deadlines are looming and crushing, and sometimes, compromises happen. And yeah, people know it's not always to the best of their ability but it's what they're able to deliver within those constraints. Once you've been on that side, you look at things with a very different countenance. There's a different set of values you place on the work that you can't get across to the critic. You roll with it and move on, trying to do better.

I'm not saying the work is better than what you see or the criticism isn't valid, but that work can't be taken in isolation.

Helvie: You also mentioned those critics who are looking to "help" you rewrite the story and "coach" the creative team. As a teacher, do you use peer review in your classroom and how do you help students avoid falling into this trap?

Zub: We break the animation program down into three years, and it's in the first year we teach them all of the technical knowledge they need to know about how things work. Then in the second year, we start pulling back a bit more from the instructor-led critique model and get the students to engage in more peer review. They now have some of the tools for analysis and they can see them better and clearer. By the third year, they not only have the ability create the work but also present it. It's really valuable. One of the important aspects of what we teach them is not only to produce but to lead and put their ideas forward.

Helvie: We focus on critiquing the work not the person in my writing classes. How do you guide your students to engage in those discussions about what did or did not work for them in their peers' art?

Zub: One of the things we talk about very early on is that when you begin to create work, you also need to develop an opinion. That opinion has to be more than just "I like it" or "I don't like it." You need to be able to point to those specific elements of the work felt well-executed or maybe disingenuous. That's really valuable and it comes top down. When we talk film or art, we always try to build that case for or against, treating both ends of the spectrum with respect. I can truly dislike something without being dismissive.

Helvie: That seems to underscore your previous point about how the criticism is delivered.

Zub: Right. There's this weird thought with some fans that people want to create garbage. Not true. It seems obvious, but no one goes into a project with the intent to make a bad story. It might have come out badly, but that wasn't the intent. There's a human behind that story.

And on a similar note, it's important to avoid overly prescribing intent. Too often I'll see critics asserting that I meant to do X, Y, or Z; the truth is nowhere near that. You know, the good thing about fandom is the sheer amount of passion. The downside is there are assumptions about the intent behind the work. That can be difficult as well.

Helvie: People in comics rarely work in single issue format though. You have to "hang on" a bit to ensure you're bringing a sort of context to the review, don't you?

Zub: Yeah, for sure. You do want to understand the purpose of the work. A 10/10 doesn't mean life-changing; it simply means it succeeded in every aspect of what it set out to accomplish and was thoroughly entertaining. The flaws were so minor they weren't even worth bringing up.

Helvie: When we look at the context, how do we attribute credit to the right members of the creative team?

Zub: There's a real lack of public understanding of how much or how little a given member of the team contributes to the comic. One time I had a fill-in artist on a title, and there were fans who were (incorrectly) giving me credit for the changes the artist made just because I was the one constant. They seemed to think I had all of this control, when that's not how it worked. And each creative team operates differently. I may have much greater control over a story on a creator-owned book but that could change when we look at work-for-hire and there's editorial input that gets factored into the story.

Helvie: This raises the issue then of whether or not the critic should even try to engage in attribution of elements of the story.

Zub: On one hand, when someone's not getting paid on a review, it's hard to come down and force them to pick out every last little thing. On the other hand, there's a part of me that also says if you're going to put something out there with your name on it, you need to put forward the best possible product. I waffle back and forth on this issue.

Obviously, the least a critic can do is identify the captions and dialogue as being the work of the writer and the visual elements as being associated with the art team. Similarly, there's absolutely no reason the art should be ignored. People often view the story as the thing they understand, so that's what they're most keen to discuss. This goes doubly so for those would-be-comic writers who want to showcase what they know. But many critics who are not artists, they can often feel out of their depths discussing.

Helvie: How much technical knowledge does the critic need to have about the art – whether they are an amateur blogger, a professional comics critic, or even a professor who's seeking to publish in more academic journals? Is *Understanding Comics* enough?

Zub: Terminology needs to be correct. There are few things worse than reading feedback where the writer has no idea about what he or she is talking about. The letterer does not create the dialogue. They're word balloons – not "floaty things." If you want to be taken seriously, take some time and be serious.

Helvie: What are the two to three most important things people need to consider when they're reviewing comics, regardless of format?

Zub: I think it's important they cover the full spectrum of story production. Let's talk about plot progression and character development. Let's dig into the art. The colors. The lettering. That's a field people know so little about. Industry pros often say that the best lettering is the kind that you never notice. It just fades into the background. When the lettering works in tandem with the art, it directs the eye and the reader moves fluidly through the story. That's the sort of observation from a critic that makes people stand up a notice that they're paying attention to the details.

Anyone can come in and tell you whether or not they liked something. It's easy to give a hot take. That's valid, but if you want to be a critic and do this with the intent to be taken seriously, it behooves you to know the form and how it works. Understand the production pipeline, but don't get caught up in prescribing blame. Speak openly about the comic as a series of pieces coming together.

Helvie: As a concluding thought, what do you think about the value of comics criticism – academic or journalistic?

Zub: People make a lot of broad assumptions about how projects get into production and the decisions made by editorial. I want to educate, and yeah, sometimes I get tired and let it lie. You can't save everyone, and people have to want to learn. If someone just wants to rant, then this isn't going to change that.

Criticism, when done well, can be valuable though. Every so often, someone throws me a curveball. It can generate ideas — or you can set it aside and decide not to address that concern. But at least you're more aware of that point of view.

José Villarubia (*Conan, Promethea, Infidel*)

Forrest C. Helvie: What are the top mistakes that you can think of that critics make when reviewing or analyzing comics?

José Villarubia: I think the top mistakes that you can think of that critics make when reviewing or analyzing comics are:

- Writing about their ideas about the character and how they should be handled, like back seat drivers telling the creative team how they should do it to please them.
- Writing about the story only.
- Writing about the art only.
- Ignoring the storytelling aspect of the work.
- Ignoring inking, coloring, lettering, design.

Helvie: What are a few of the most important things you would want everyone who is writing about comics – whether students, journalists, or critics – to be more aware of?

Villarubia: There are three things people writing about comics need to know about. The most important aspect of comics is not the story of the art, but how both blend together. Second, if you are uneducated in art theory and history or the fundamentals of writing, consider taking a class or at least read some books on the topic. Finally, learn comics history and learn about world comics. Make sure you acquire a solid knowledge of the field before issuing opinions.

Helvie: Are there any examples of people or places who you feel are "getting it right" in terms of writing about and analyzing comics?

Villarubia: There are several writers that do it well, but no "place: where I think this happens consistently.

Helvie: Do you read reviews of your work or critical analyses of comics you've helped create?

Villarubia: All the time.

Helvie: Can you tell me about the harshest – but more fairly written – review you received? What made it fair and why did you give it credence?

Villarubia: I honestly don't remember. I am pleased that most reviews that bother to mention my work are very positive.

Helvie: As someone who works with students in either creative writing or art classes, how often do you have students engage in peer review?

Villarubia: Every week.

Helvie: What are some of the guidelines you put in place to help your students provide their peers with useful feedback and constructive criticism?

Villarubia: Comment on the positive aspects of what they have done so far, and make suggestions about those that could use improvement.

Helvie: One of the frustrations often expressed by writers and artists centers on the critic explaining what he or she would have done to make the story better. Do you find your students doing this when commenting on one another's work? What problems can this create when they engage in this type of feedback?

Villarubia: Students are not professionals. There is no comparison. Students are a "work in progress" and need constructive feedback. I think that professionals don't. They should be evaluated, but not instructed, since the reviewer is not in a position of authority, artistically or professionally, over the creative team.

Helvie: How do you help your students better focus their peer critiques?

Villarubia: I give them a set of rubrics to keep their evaluation and critique grounded.

Helvie: What are the most basic elements of line work / inking / coloring / lettering that any critics should be aware of? Given your expertise in coloring, I'd really love to hear your thoughts in this area, but please feel free to touch upon the rest as well.

Villarubia: A rudimentary knowledge of color theory would be welcome. An understanding of the effects of color in storytelling is ideal.

Helvie: We understand comics are created through a variety of different contributions – not just between the writer and artist/s but also the editor. Are there times when you've had your work critiqued – positively or negatively – and it was actually something someone else from your team did? How should critics handle this? We're in a period with comics where there is a real need to credit all members of the team, but what do you think is a viable means of doing this when unsure of each member's exact contributions?

Villarubia: The credits should specify what the attributions are and reflect what each person did. Sometimes I got critiqued for things in the colors that were not my decisions. That is fine with me, but if the reviewer has questions, they can contact the creative team.

Helvie: Is there a fundamental difference between traditional v. digital art that the critic needs to be aware of?

Villarubia: No. They should just evaluate the finished product.

Helvie: How would you say form helps to convey more than just plot (i.e. tone, mood, theme, etc)?

Villarubia: Obviously everything other than plot creates tone, mood, theme... script layout, drawings, acting, lighting, color, pacing, rendering, texture, lettering, they all should work in unison.

Hannah Means-Shannon (former EIC Bleeding Cool, former Associate Editor for Dark Horse Comics, current Executive Editor at Comicon.com and Managing Editor at Waxwork Comics)

Forrest C. Helvie: What are the top mistakes that you can think of that critics make when reviewing or analyzing comics?

Hannah Means-Shannon: The most basic and obvious mistake that happens across the board, whether on a superficial level or on a deeper critical level, is the false assumption that the comic that one holds in one's hands is by default the product of a single unifying creative vision. This is a massive obstacle to overcome for critics coming from a literary tradition and attempting to analyze comics. It undermines one's ability to approach comics conceptually or speak about comics in appropriate critical terms, since the terms used will reveal an underlying bias.

This assumption has onion-like layers that can only be stripped away over time through working closely alongside the medium and researching widely. Unfortunately, a student-critic can be informed of the number of creative team-members who contributed to a comic, and even understand their roles, but still fall back on this assumption in order to speak about the comic as a whole. The best way to approach this problem is no doubt to apply very distinctive critical lenses that focus on certain aspects of the comic in question and arrive at a mosaic-like series of critiques about the same work in order to demonstrate just how separate the creative choices being made actually are.

Of course, there are comics which are the work of a single creative vision, and no doubt they deserve just as much critical attention, but in this case, applying the different critical lenses to a unified work should be illuminating as well, casting the creator in the different roles necessary to produce the final work.

Helvie: What are a few things you would want everyone who is writing about comics – whether students, journalists, or critics – to be more aware of?

Means-Shannon: As strange as it may sound, one factor that could be very helpful for readers and critics to be more aware of would be the role of time in the composition of comics. Whether being made aware of the rapid pace of production and communication between team members on single-issue comics being published on a monthly or bimonthly basis, or the rather vast swaths of time now playing a role in the creation of graphic novels for the book market. To fail to differentiate between these different circumstances when analyzing comics can only lead to inaccuracies. Regarding single issues, the critic may fail to praise the depth of composition accomplished under extreme time constraints and instead focus on minor imperfections prompted by the schedule. In the case of long timeframes, the critic may comment on a book lacking immediate relevance or failing to address current issues when the book was, in fact, created years before due to the needs of the book market.

Secondly, it's very unlikely that readers or critics, academic or journalistic, have a solid enough understanding of the role of publishers in determining what comics reach readers and in what vein. It's hard to keep in mind just how deeply influential the world of business and money-making are on one's favorite comic that somehow manages to address an urgent theme one feels one needs to see more of in our culture. Unfortunately, publishers are not all that transparent with the public or critics regarding their processes for choosing books for publication, choosing creative teams (where appropriate) or shaping the content or goals of the work in question. And yet it is an area which would significantly impact comics journalism and academic critique if more were known. The only remedy for this lack of information is to encourage greater transparency from publishers and greater awareness from critics, including a basic understanding of how the publishing world functions and what factors might impact the final product. To give a very basic case example, a journalist reviewer might assume that the plot structure of a licensed comic was created by the writer of said comic and praise it symmetry. The actual creation of that plot structure might have come from an EIC, CCO, or even the license owner of the comic as part of the publishing deal. Operating under false assumptions does not help critical writing.

Lastly, comics journalism and comics studies are often sadly lacking in an understanding of the role of the human element in the production of comics. In an attempt to present a cool critical appraisal, one can veer far from appreciating comics as the production of actual human beings operating, often without a great deal of training and with pressures of many kinds, to produce works in a medium they love. The human element is strongly influenced by the rise and fall of the market, making livelihood difficult, overwork, the lack of labor unions for freelance work, and lack of health care to provide in times of medical need. These factors make work in comics tenuous at times, result in flawed or delayed work in monthly books, or projects that never reach completion. Criticism falls hard on these situations in comics journalism and in comics scholarship these realities are rarely addressed. And yet anyone who works in a field adjacent to comics should be aware of these factors and failing to appreciate them fails to support the survival of the medium through its creators.

Helvie: It sounds like contextualizing the comic in terms of its production plays an important role in its evaluation.

Given their role in the production process, let's talk about comics editors. Editors are often seen as background players when it comes to creating comics; yet, they play an integral role in the shaping of not only the comic's story but often the team as well. How much awareness of the editor's role in this process should critics, scholars, and/or press possess?

Means-Shannon: This can only devolve into a matter of opinion, since this has never been handled uniformly in the publishing industry. Each company and each type of publication follows different traditions and comics publishing has continued to be equally diverse. One possible approach that might be helpful would be the following scenario: The publisher should celebrate the creative team behind a single issue comic or book in their PR and media cycle, making sure that the creators can build a career off of their name branding in the future. In turn, the creative team should be apologists for the role of the editor and represent their interaction with editorial accurately, since each project is different. For instance, on some projects, the creative teams are highly efficient with their own team-leads and the editor merely acts as an emissary between the creative team and the publisher, while on many books, creator owned or licensed, the editor may have a much more involved role in shaping the comic to meet the needs of the publisher or in developing the comic to best serve the creative team. The massive variation from project to project in the role of editor means that awareness of the media would have to be on a project-by-project basis.

Traditionally in comics, it seems that editors often think their work speaks for itself and have maintained a great deal of silence about their role, and in many cases you can see a fine and distinguished list of projects that helps to outline an editor's achievements over time. However, a general silence about editing comics and what the role actually entails results in misconceptions and perhaps prejudice in comics journalism and even comics scholarship. Blanket silence isn't helpful anymore in the Internet age. As a younger generation of editors emerges, they are becoming more active at conventions and in speaking from a personal perspective online, but there is still a long way to go in opening up the editorial role to public understanding. As to how much awareness critics should have of the editorial role, ideally they should have as much understanding as possible when addressing a particular project. A basic understanding of whether an editor was more involved in formal aspects of editing, like quality control of punctuation or resolution of artwork, or was instead involved in deeper aspects of establishing clear plot-structure or dialogue coherency as well, would be a good start.

Helvie: In perhaps a bigger picture sense, what value as a whole do you see comics criticism possessing in relation to the comics publishing industry? (Again, academic criticism, online news / journalism coverage, etc)

Means-Shannon: The answer to this is deceptively simple, but in short, the value of comics criticism to the comics publishing industry is immense since the medium is young. Just as any and all stars visible on a cloudy night were valuable to mariners in past ages. It may seem like plenty has been written about comics so far, just from visiting online sites or noting bibliographies on established comics studies courses, but in comparison to the varied writing that supports the study and critique of other mediums, this is a tiny amount. For one thing, the cultural legitimacy of comics is still being established, particularly in Britain and the USA, while some nations have progressed further in this regard. The future of comics publishing is still, frankly, in danger of becoming a very limited boutique market. The more varied perspectives are being recorded in response to the comics medium, the greater the medium's chance for survival. Criticism brings readers to comics from varied disciplines, and provides readers with the tools to embark on their own investigations. Without existing comics criticism, I would never have read the complete works of Alan Moore, Neil Gaiman, Warren Ellis, and many more, or become a comics scholar. Without existing comics journalism, I would never have become a writer about comics who has thereby recruited many more readers both through online platforms and conventions. Will publishers make more money if comics journalism and comics scholarship exist? Absolutely, they will. Just ask the retailers who receive pre-order numbers on comics after articles run online or the librarians who are ordering graphic novels for their university or public libraries.

If instead we are speaking about the impact of criticism on the actual production of the contents of comics, there is also plenty of value to consider.

For instance, publishers blunder into plot configurations or character assumptions all the time that are simply not acceptable to a progressive comics-reading audience. Sometimes in the rush to get something published, things that may seem obvious are overlooked by publishers, and comics journalism should play a role in pointing out the need for change. The reverse is also true. Publishers are often risk-averse, meaning changing with the times is hard for them if they don't fully understand there is an audience for new and developing genres or themes in comics. So if a publisher tentatively makes positive steps toward reaching an emerging audience, comics journalism should be responsive in discussing and supporting those steps, which will make publishers more confident to take such steps in the future. In short, the constructive criticism and vocal support of comics journalism should be of value to comics publishers and can only result in more successful sales figures for them.

Helvie: As a reviewer / critic, what was your primary intent? We often hear a debate about how criticism should push artists to create better art; others believe the aim is to showcase good art. Where do you fall on this issue?

Means-Shannon: My primary intent as a reviewer or academic critic has always been to contribute to the longevity of the comics medium. The most direct way to do that, it seems to me, is to open wider channels between the creators and the readers for better mutual understanding. That way the creators find their readers and the readers better appreciate creators and continue to support their work. Within that, my goal is primarily to celebrate contributions to the comics medium that have qualities which may prove to be of enduring cultural value, whether from a literary or artistic standpoint. A balanced critical evaluation may point out room for improvement while appreciating a work's positive qualities, of course.

I do not primarily review or critique comics in order to encourage improvement from the creative teams in question, however very occasionally if I perceive a work to be actually destructive to the forward progress of the medium, whether due to explicit or implicit content or style, I will write a purely critical piece attempting to point out why this is the case. I reserve this type of corrective writing for comics journalism and have not yet written an academic article that is wholly an attempt to improve the medium. It seems to me that if improvement is a goal, comics journalism is a more direct way to reach the creative teams making comics than through the academy. I would add that discussing comics in a "corrective" way is, however, entirely appropriate in the classroom since it may serve as a springboard for a great deal of discussion about the medium.

Helvie: As a review/ critics or news editor, did you ever encounter issues of professional misconduct (either people using their writing to go after creators, or on the other side, attempting curry favor with creators or publishers)? How can writers avoid these pitfalls in their work?

Means-Shannon: It's difficult to answer this question without appearing to be deliberately shocking, but that's not my intent. As someone who has self-edited as a contributing editor, and supervised scores of comics journalists in their work through the role of editor-in-chief, I have spent about twenty percent of my time in those roles concerned about the possibility of gray areas or in overtly cracking down on misconduct. By that I mean that this is an incredibly problematic area when it comes to comics journalism. I don't mean to say that comics journalists are somehow less ethical than journalists in other fields, but I do see that the nature of the publishing industry, the growth of conventions, and the floodgates that have opened in recent years into fandoms previously under-represented in the press, have all contributed to a chaotic situation where journalists or bloggers receive very little guidance and can naively stumble into potential minefields. Since the divide between being a fan and being a journalist has become increasingly blurred, it's no surprise that many writers don't maintain clear enough boundaries under pressure.

Helvie: Are there are a few areas you can point to where you see this happening most frequently?

Means-Shannon: Being general probably doesn't help answer this question, so I'll attempt to be specific about a few areas. The sad truth to emphasize is that the writers who found themselves in these situations discussed below did not think it compromised the integrity of their work until the problems were pointed out and explained to them.

Firstly, writers selling interviews to various media outlets after misrepresenting to the creators in question the nature of the interviews they were conducting or where the interview would appear to the public. That included dividing up interviews into smaller pieces and selling them to multiple sites in order to make a greater profit.

Secondly, using connections gained under one guise to fuel another, perhaps more personal project. For instance, presenting themselves as a writer for a particular media outlet, conducting an interview, and then spending part of that time talking creators into appearing as guests on a show or podcast that would result in personal profit. In other words, using one role as entrance to another role with said creator.

Thirdly, accepting and encouraging special treatment from comic publishers in the form of free merchandise, free food, drink, entertainment, or accommodation at conventions in the understanding that the writer would represent the publisher's work favorably in the media.

Lastly, writers avoiding pushback from publishers who might become disgruntled by publishing only favorable articles in order to make sure they could access high-profile creators to further their journalistic work. You'll notice the last two in this list reflect a high degree of complicity from publishers, and that area is a particular danger to less experienced writers.

Helvie: While it may seem obvious to some readers, why exactly are these issues problematic especially for those newer writers seeking to break into the business of comics journalism?

Means-Shannon: To point out the salient elements here for the purpose of showing how writers can avoid mistakes, in items one and two, the writer is failing to present an honest and clear account of their intentions to the creators they are working with when setting up an interview or discussion. That is never acceptable, since creators interact with journalists in good faith and make agreements based upon how they believe their thoughts and ideas are going to be presented to the public. Agreements should be made ahead of time and the writer should not deviate from those plans however tempted they might be to alter them. For absolute clarity, which is best to avoid any gray areas, the single publication outlet should be established beforehand rather than attempting to "shop" interviews around to various sites afterward.

The latter two points, as I mentioned, show that fault can exist on both sides of the equation, whether from writer or publisher. In these circumstances, publishers might genuinely feel generous in giving writers free books and merchandise in thanks for their fandom or to encourage them to review the products, or there may exist a gray area where positive reviews are expected. At what point does this gifting become excessive? Accepting merchandise to review in moderation is certainly acceptable, but writers need to draw a line at what might seem overly generous gestures. When it comes to free food, drink, or entertainment, one must ask oneself, are many other journalists also being hosted? If so, the likelihood is that accepting a drink or dinner invitation is fair. Is a writer being singled out for special treatment? If so, the writer needs to think carefully about accepting those gestures from a publisher. Lastly, a writer should never accept travel payment or accommodation at a convention from a publisher. It would compromise clear judgement in reporting the publisher's presence at the convention or in future writing.

Helvie: Up to this point, it seems more of the onus falls on the individual journalist; however, the final item falls more in the lane of responsibility of the publisher, no?

Means-Shannon: Regarding the final item, some writers might fear pushback from publishers that results in limited access to creators, and unfortunately, a number of publishers are known to use these methods to control the media message created by journalists. For instance, if a writer reviews a new book negatively, a publisher might blacklist them from access to any of the creators exclusive to said publisher. This is not an exaggeration and is sadly, a common thing. It creates an undue pressure on journalists to maintain a good relationship with publishers through generating solely positive media exposure. It is understandable that writers would be fearful of this scenario. A writer needs to measure the cost of capitulating to this pressure. What are they really getting out of this relationship? If accessing major creators means a purely publisher-controlled outcome in the articles that result in this access, then it is not worth it. Writers needs to ask themselves if personal fandom for particular creators and a desire to spend time talking with those creators is undermining their ability to operate with journalistic freedom. Are they therefore putting their fandom ahead of their journalistic role?

Helvie: How would you advise newer writers to deal with these circumstances?

Means-Shannon: In the kind of chaotic milieu characteristic of comics journalism at this time, the only way for writers to avoid slipping into these pressurizing situations is through mentorship which offers clear situation-based guidance, and through maintaining absolute clarity in their professional interactions with creators and publishers.

Beyond the Printed Page

Comics see publication in more than just the standard print format. Likewise, criticism and discussion of comics also finds itself published in more than just the written word. These final two articles take a close look at how to effectively analyze and review webtoons or webcomics along with recommendations for how to interview and discuss comics with creators involved either in a podcast format or a traditional interview discussion.

Quick Hits and Deep Dives: Conducting Podcast Interviews

by Brian LeTendre

I have been fortunate enough to interview a good many comic creators in the ten-plus years that I produced and co-hosted the Secret Identity podcast with my partner Matt Herring. Each interview was a new opportunity to learn more about the medium we love and the people who make the magic. But podcast interviews are a different animal than print or video interviews. The format and focus of your podcast are going to inform the type of creator interviews you do, and I tend to categorize podcast interviews into two major categories: Quick Hits and Deep Dives. We're going to focus a bit more on Deep Dive interviews here, but I'll take a minute or two to talk about Quick Hits first.

As the name implies, a Quick Hit interview is generally a short conversation with a comic creator, anywhere from five to fifteen minutes. We did a lot of these for Secret Identity (we called them Creator Spotlights), and most were conducted at comic conventions. The shorter length is driven by the fact that the creator just doesn't have time for a longer interview. Therefore, the approach to this type of interview is much more focused. Many times, the Quick Hit interview is cold as well, meaning the interviewer hasn't had time to prep. It might be with a creator you just met, about a book that caught your eye while you were walking through artist alley.

For Quick Hits, my advice is to have a focus and stick to it. If you know the creator's work, pick one aspect of it and make your short interview about that (their new project, your favorite storyline, etc.). If you don't know their work, spend a few minutes talking to them before you ask for an interview, and find your angle through that conversation. It shouldn't just be about the elevator pitch for their book. Find a common ground, be it the love of a particular genre, an influence of theirs you are a fan of, or even their experience at the con itself. Go into the interview with a focus, so you're not just putting all of the pressure on them to sell their book to your audience through the interview. While listeners do want to hear about the work, they also want to feel like they connected with the creator. That's your job in the Quick Hit – give them a little window into who this person is that created the thing your listeners like. Most importantly though – always end your interview by thanking the creator for their time and asking them where people can find out more about them and their work.

My go-to questions for Quick Hit interviews (especially if it's the first time I'm seeing their work) involve the creative process behind the particular project we are talking about. I ask about how the original idea came about, how it's changed, the lifecycle of the project, the creative back and forth with the other people working on the book (if there are other people), etc. Between the elevator pitch for the project and the process questions, you can fill five to ten minutes easy, and come out with a well-rounded discussion.

Deep Dives are longer form interviews, which certainly could happen at a show, but will more likely occur when you have someone guest on your podcast. These are discussions that you can prep for ahead of time, and you absolutely should. My goal with the Deep Dive is to gain insight into the creative process and the creators themselves – from their origin story, to the genesis of a project, to all of the little creative decisions they are making along the way. The Deep Dive gives you, the creator, and the listener more time to breathe than the Quick Hit does. It should be a comfortable conversation, more discussion than question and answer session.

For me, the three parts of this process are securing the interview, prepping for the interview, and conducting the interview. We'll focus on the latter two here, but when it comes to securing a guest for the podcast, my biggest piece of advice is to be humble and respectful. Most comic creators have a preferred means of being contacted for interviews, and it isn't to tweet at them in front of the whole world. Check their website for contact information, be clear in your request for an interview, and realize it is perfectly fine for a creator to say no. Not everyone wants to be recorded for a podcast, and that's fine. You want to interview creators that are comfortable and who your listeners will get something out of listening to during the discussion.

Prepping for an interview starts with familiarizing yourself with the work of the creator. Maybe you can't read everything they've ever done, but you should certainly be familiar enough with their work that it will not limit the conversation. If the creator's current project is their first, you should absolutely be familiar with it. When the project is already released, I purchase a copy (unless a review copy has already been offered). If you're writing for a larger site, they usually have PR contacts with publishers and can get you a review copy if you need it. Another bonus of the project already being out is that you can read reviews and check different sites/social media to see what discussion is already happening around the book. It's a great way to generate interview questions.

I also track down and listen to any other podcast interviews the creator has done for two reasons. First, to get a feel for how they present, and second, to filter out questions they get asked all the time. I don't want to bore my guest by asking them the same questions they get everywhere else.

This brings me to the origin story issue. If it's the first time you've interviewed a particular creator, then it's fine to ask some of the usual questions about how they got their start and things like that. But in my experience, these are often the least interesting questions for a creator to answer, and there are things you can do to make them more interesting. If you've done your homework, you should be familiar with their origin story already. Take one aspect of it, and build a few questions around it. Create a jumping off point for discussion rather than making the creator stand in front of the class and tell everyone about themselves.

Don't forget, you can provide a lot of that bio when you introduce the interview on your podcast. The less time you spend on that during the interview, the more time you have to dive into their work and the process behind it.

I like to go into a Deep Dive interview with an outline of topics I want to cover. I share this list with the creator ahead of time. This gives them an opportunity to add anything they want to make sure we touch on, or remove anything they don't feel like talking about. Which is a good segue into conducting the interview.

A big thing to remember when having a guest on your podcast is that the listeners want to hear them talk about the things they make. They hear you all the time. So, keep the focus on your guest. Now, that doesn't mean you should just fire questions at them and then shut up, it just means that you should be steering the conversation back to the creator and their work. Be wary of needless digression that is focused on you, not the creator.

Another golden rule when it comes to podcast interviews is that you want your guest to be comfortable. Make the process as easy as possible for them. Remember to give them the outline of questions/topics ahead of time. Work around their schedule. Provide a good estimate of what the time commitment will be (for example, I might only record a 30-minute interview, but I want to block off at least 45 minutes for chatting, wrap-up, etc.) And you should definitely spend some time talking to your guest before you actually hit that record button, so they're not "on" the second you connect with them.

One of the biggest things you can do to make a creator comfortable is to be comfortable yourself. This is easier said than done, and it's made more difficult if you're doing an audio-only interview, as you have no ability to read body language or facial reactions. But if you're coming across as relaxed, prepared and genuinely interested from the time you start talking, you'll set a great tone for the discussion. My advice around this is to practice as much as possible. Record some discussions over Skype {Google Hangouts, etc.}. You'll hear when you're interrupting, you'll fine tune your style, and you'll be more comfortable when you have to record with someone you don't know well.

Once you get into the actual interview, you want to "find the flow" as soon as possible. Within the first couple questions/topics, you want to settle into a nice back and forth where your guest is doing the majority of the talking, and you are moving through questions/topics in a way that keeps the conversation rolling along. One of the best ways to keep a discussion flowing is to be an active listener. If you're too busy looking at your list of topics, or trying to think of the next question to ask, you're not really listening to your guest, and that makes for a choppy interview. Every time they speak, they're giving you something to build on, so listen. The interview will begin to steer itself, as opportunities for follow-up begin to present themselves.

For example, let's say I'm interviewing a comic writer about the popular comic *Super Awesome Guy*. The writer is currently working with an artist who is well known for drawing that character over the years, and the writer is talking about how amazing it is to be working with that artist. I've got several opportunities here. I could ask about the writer's favorite issues of *Super Awesome Guy* that the legendary artist has drawn over the years. I could ask about what the creative process is like with that legendary artist. I could ask about other artists that the writer has either worked with or would like to work with. Each of those questions and answers will present new opportunities.

And this brings me back to the outline. If you start with a good outline for the discussion, you'll have plenty of starting points. If you're an active listener, every time you throw a topic out there you'll have plenty of opportunities to keep the flow going with follow-up questions. The best interviews are the ones that just continue to organically build from topic to topic. They have a great flow, they're fun to listen to, and they're comfortable for both the interviewer and the interviewee. This is a great advantage that podcast interviews have over print interviews, and you should leverage that advantage as much as possible.

As we head down the home stretch here, there are a couple more things I want to mention. First, you should always be mindful of your time, and come right out of the gate with your best questions. You want to make sure you get those questions in – there's nothing worse than ending an interview and wishing you had asked something. Know when you need to start wrapping things up, and adjust the conversation accordingly. You want to make sure you leave time at the end for not only thanking your guest, but making sure to promote them and letting people know where they can support the creator and their work.

My last overall tip for anyone conducting interviews is to be humble, and be real. Always be respectful of your guest's time, and remember the interview is about them, not you. Do not try to be something you're not when you're interviewing people. I interview people the way I would talk to them if we were hanging out. I get excited about people's work, I'm fascinated by the creative process, and I love to get people talking about their passion. You can hear that in the interviews I do.

If you develop a reputation of being someone that people want to talk to, word gets around. Creators will be more likely to grant interviews when other creators are vouching for you because of the good work you do and how you conduct yourself.

Can Someone Review My Web Comic?:
Strategies to Evaluate and Criticize Web Comics

by Hervé Saint-Louis

Reviews matter for web comic creators. Popular web comic platforms such as Comic Fury and Tapastic dedicate large discussion spaces for the review of web comics created by members. In fact, web cartoonists continually struggle to gain reviews from peers and readers possibly more than their traditional book publishing counterparts.

There are so many web comics and creators of all levels that the comic press dedicated to comic reviews ignore much of the material from web cartoonists. While professionals and amateurs of all ages use web comics to deploy their work, many cartoonists use the medium as a testing ground to test new comic ideas and to learn about sequential art production. These cartoonists create web comics specifically for the Web.

An important problem when reviewing web comics is how to manage serials that span several years and pages. For example, "long-form" web comics are multi-page serials that could be anywhere between 50, 300 pages or more. How can reviewers assess storytelling, line work, color, and lettering in web comics? How can they approach them without constantly comparing them to print comics? For example, one form of web comics, the 'webtoon' uses a vertical format that affects a comic page's composition.

Webtoons

Webtoons are web comics created specifically for the Web. They are vertical comics read through scrolling. Webtoons explore the continuous format first espoused by Scott McCloud (2000) in *Reinventing Comics*. Webtoons are a response to the consumption of comics on mobile devices. They attempt to solve the problem of how can a reader read a comic on a limited space with as few clicks and interactions with an interface.

The use of space in webtoons affects the storytelling, line work, colors and lettering. For example the space between panels, best known as the gutter (McCloud 1994), does not necessarily exist in webtoons. A continuous flow of morphing lines or degrading colors may meld one frame into another. The effect is similar to how cartoon animators create travelling shots and pans using one large background used within the camera view in animated productions. The lettering may be used to connect different panels while floating captions disconnected from artwork almost play the role of voice-overs linking disparate pockets of visual space.

The first element that a webtoon reviewer needs to notice and then evaluate is how the effect of closure is used creatively in a comic. Closure is the process of readers filling story gaps from the gutters between comic panels (McCloud 1994). How does the cartoonist use the transitions between panels creatively? Is she relying on the same tricks seen in many other comics or is she innovating her play with closure? Are the gaps in space too wide between elements as to create an island effect with tenuous connections between captions, foreground and background elements?

Are the elements within a webtoon placed vertically in a composition that encourages the reader to jump from one component to another? Is it more work for the reader to surf through a continuous page than using a traditional page layout? All of these questions are related to the storytelling skills of the cartoonist.

Storytelling

Other web comics that rely on layouts closer to print comics have different storytelling problems related to use of space. Print comics rely on a few page-based storytelling features, such as the splash page and the double-page spread. These storytelling devices are used for dramatic effects to highlight important story elements such as the conflict that triggers the action of a story, in the case of the splash page or a climactic moment, when pencillers use double-page spreads.

The splash page and the double-page spread do not exist independently from the rest of the comic. They are part of the flow of a story that creates narrative peaks and lows. In a web comic, the page is often a standalone element. Because of their episodic nature that borrows from comic strips, web comic pages often appear as individual segments that need to sustain reader interest and interaction for indeterminate lengths of time.

A web cartoonist may update his web comic once a week. For that whole week, this page has to sustain the narrative appetite of readers. If using a splash page to introduce important elements, the cartoonist can easily rely on supporting pages introduced prior. However, for a weekly installment, no supporting page will help decrease the narrative peak generated by the splash page. The web cartoonist has to be conscious of this storytelling conundrum.

As for double-page spreads, they can exist but at the same time, the cartoonist must either split the page in two or feature twice as much visual elements in the space usually reserved for one. Publishing a double-page spread as two separate pages is awkward. Stuffing twice as much information in the same space with a double-page spread makes the page crowed, and captions smaller, and harder to read.

Another way the cartoonist can treat the web comic page is as a whole unit that while it is part of a series of pages, an issue, or a chapter, is meant to be read independently. The flow of a story often spills to subsequent pages in print comics. A sequence of a superhero pursuing a villain may spill on several pages with little interruptions. As mentioned above, multi page story flows that are interrupted due to the episodic nature of web comics can be problematic for readers.

When a page is treated as a whole unit, there is a short narrative sequence contained within the entire page, even when part of a larger sequence. For example, a pursuit between a superhero and a villain can focus only on one aspect of the chase, like jumping from one building to another. Everything related to the jump would be self-contained to one page. The next page could focus on another aspect of the whole sequence, such as climbing down a fire escape. Web comic reviewers should understand techniques used by cartoonists to attenuate the negative effects of episodic storytelling.

- Are they splash pages or double-page spreads in the comic?
- How were these elements integrated to facilitate the reading experience of the reader, even if the book is meant to be printed in the future?
- Do individual pages tell a standalone story, allowing for updates appearing over time?

Line Work

One of the greatest attributes of web comics is the opportunity for readers to preview the evolution of a budding cartoonist in one concentrated body of work over time. Many amateur and semi-professional cartoonists start their web comics with rough doodles that improve over time. As a reviewer, recognizing the development of a cartoonist and addressing this aspect of their work is a great opportunity to offer insightful criticism and evaluation.

Because of their commercial nature, print comics publishers often filter out nascent cartoonists who may not master all the basic skills to be featured in a project. At most, short stories, fill-in issues, and obscure publishers provide a training ground for emerging cartoonists. Rarely, as was the case with Doug Mahnke's work on Dark Horse Comics' *The Mask* (1993) and *The Mask Returns* (1994), will readers be able to witness the growth of an artist over a single body of printed work.

Web comics, notwithstanding self-published comics, offer the best opportunity for reviewers to notice and evaluate the development of a cartoonist. But reviewers have to be strategic about what constitutes a suitable sample of a web comic under review. As mentioned above, some web comics span hundreds and even in some cases, thousands of pages. Are rough pages created in the initial years of a web cartoonists' career as relevant in a review as their latest and professional-level work?

One approach reviewers can use to tackle long-form comics is to focus on one theme from the comic or story arcs. Many web comics have clearly stated chapters and story arcs which are the equivalent of single issues, mini-series, graphic novels. Reviewing the entirety of a long-form comic of several hundred pages is the equivalent of reviewing the body of work of a cartoonist such as Dave Sims, the creator of *Cerebus* (1998) in one review. Such a review would be superficial, unless it tackled a specific theme throughout the series.

What are the periods of continuity and changes in the comic's line work? For example, when did the cartoonist abandon her use of animé-inspired eyes to something more personal? Was the change sudden? Was it experimental? Was it a shortcut that quickly became a stylistic trick? Were there parallel changes in her storytelling, or page layouts?

Color

A way to understand the work of a cartoonist is to see how he optimizes his work over time. For example, web comics created by semi-professionals and amateurs seem over-colored compared to print comics. Unlike print comics where productions, time and budgets limit the expenses spent on colors, web cartoonists often do not constrain their comics' coloring. Their coloring may be as intricate as marquee projects from top-tier publishers.

Eventually, time restrictions, and other life constraints may force the cartoonist to optimize his coloring to remain productive and on schedule. These moments show an evolution in the creative strategies and priorities of the cartoonist. A similar process is a cartoonist changing his comic from a black and white project to one with colors. Astute reviewers will recognize these moments in the development of the cartoonist and uncover the motivations for the changes.

- How does the cartoonist use color?
- Is the color palette simple or complex?
- How did the comic change if it went from black and white to color?

Lettering

Whereas a professional letterer will optimize the use of space and text, the web cartoonist, or even the writer of a creative team, may not show as much control over the appearance and the placement of captions in a page. In such cases, their voices are less edited, and show much about their inexperience and their intent with the web comics that they create.

- Inexperienced web comic creators often do their own lettering unlike print comics.
- The captions (the written text) within the bubbles often use non comic fonts.
- The captions often encroach or touch the edges of the bubbles or the narrative boxes not allowing the text to breathe.
- Amateur cartoonists often add many captions and bubbles within one panel instead of spreading them over several panels. They try to explain everything at once.
- If written by hand, the captions may not be legible.

I argue that many budding web comic creators are obsessed with stories that they have to tell, or quirks and ideas that they want to develop. The medium attracted many of them because of the lack of compromises and production barriers. Professional lettering may not be a priority for these creators whose focus may be on stories and illustrations.

Many web cartoonists stuff their pages with captions explaining everything about their characters and their stories, in just a few pages, forgetting that they have an unlimited canvas to expand their ideas. Their desire to be understood, and relatable is so strong that often, their comics become text walls and an archipelago of bubbles without logical connection and proper edits.

Reviewers should pay attention to how the lettering is performed in a web comic as it can help assess the experience and motivations of its creators. It is, I argue, the same insecurity that prompts so many web cartoonists to seek so much feedback for their work from peers and readers.

Conclusion

Storytelling, line work, color, and lettering are the core blocks in both web and print comics. The site where cartoonists play with these elements is the comic page. Web comics use space differently than print comics. When readers interact with a print comic, they have access to preceding and subsequent pages. Unless the comic is a one page gag, the last page that the reviewer will review in a web comic will probably end awkwardly until the cartoonist can post the next installment.

Yet, web comics offer readers and jaded reviewers an endless resource where they can sample the work of professional and amateur creators. Web comics have become a testing ground for new comics, helping creators build large audiences before committing to printing their work. They offer reviewers an important insight into the raw creative forces of unfiltered and unrestricted of cartoonists.

Works Cited

Arcudi, John, and Doug Mahnke. 1993. *The Mask.* Edited by Kij Johnson. Milwaukie, Oregon: Dark Horse Comics.

—. 1994. *The Mask Returns.* Edited by Kij Johnson and John Weeks. Milwaukie, Oregon: Dark Horse Comics.

McCloud, Scott. 2000. *Reinventing Comics.* New York, New York: Paradox Press.

—. 1994. *Understanding Comics: The Invisible Art.* New York: HarperPerennial.

Sim, Dave. 1998. *Cerebus.* Windsor: Aardvark-Vanaheim.

Afterword

by Andy Schmidt

I'm a teacher. And I teach about comics.

As a teacher, as someone who is hopefully helping creators tell their stories to the best of their abilities, the calling is to make comics better across the board. A better industry to work in, a more powerful storytelling medium, and creators who can take on journeys we never dreamed of.

And if I've learned one thing from all of my students, it's that there is no set way to tell a story. The process – an individual's process – must evolve or it will become stagnant and stagnation is the one thing none of us can afford.

And that's what I think Forrest gets right in this book, above all, he never tries to prescribe *how* one must analyze the story. This book provides the background and context and all the tools that you will likely need – but it doesn't tell you what "good" is.

If you've made it his far, and I'm glad you did, then you're probably never going to look at a comic the same way again. And that's okay.

Ultimately, Forrest and all of the contributors to this book, understand the need for analysis in our industry – but more importantly – the need for competent and reflective and thoughtful as well as thought-provoking analysis.

Because like the best teachers I've known, Forrest and those he's assembled understand that comic creation and analysis is a feedback loop. The better analysis we get on comics created means we should make better comics because we learn from the analysis, which in turn leads to better and deeper analysis and so on.

The importance of thoughtful and exploratory analysis within the medium of comics is an integral part of the evolution of comics. It's only through analysis and introspection that we can move beyond the creators we are today and into the creators we are becoming.

A book like this one understands that evolution both of content but also of analysis is integral to the continued growth, creatively, of the medium and industry in which many of spend the majority of our waking hours.

I personally thank all involved in this impressive book and hope that reviewers across the internet and new sites and magazines as well as students in classrooms at all levels give it a long and good read. Together, we'll make comics better. And this is a great place to start.

About the Contributors

Editor **Forrest C. Helvie** lives in Connecticut with his wife and two sons where he is chair and professor of developmental English at Norwalk Community College. His literary interests are broad-ranging from medieval Arthurian to 19th-century American, and most importantly, pedagogy, comics studies, and superheroes. In addition to academic publications, he writes a variety of comic short stories to include his own children's comic series, *Whiz Bang & Amelia the Adventure Bear.* He regularly writes for Sequart and reviews comics for Newsarama. Forrest can also be found on Twitter (@forrest_helvie) discussing all things comics related.

Will Allred is a writer, professor, and technologist. He created and wrote Diary of Night for BloodFire Studios, oversaw the successful Kickstarter to collect the series, contributed to the Eisner-nominated Comics through Time and multiple other academic books on comics, and is writing a second novel. Will received his Ph.D. in English from the University of Arkansas and is a longtime member of the nonprofit Grand Comics Database Project, having served for several years on its Board of Directors. Will is an avid reader and is a lifelong fan of the comics medium. He loves learning new things and enjoys teaching and spending time with his wife and twin sons.

El Anderson is a freelance comic editor, whose projects include such titles as *Errand Boys*, *Tata de Rambo*, and the Eisner-nominated *Contact High.* Between gigs she practices law and works to cultivate a diverse and welcoming comic community. Her website is www.femmesinthefridge.com, and she can be found talking too much about comics on Twitter @femmesinfridges.

Christine Atchison is a freshly-minted, early career researcher who completed her Ph.D. at Kingston University London in 2021. Her research combines three of her greatest passions – comics, culture, and people. She has had the opportunity to present her work at international conferences including the American Academy of Religion, the Canadian Society for the Study of Comics, and the Annual International Conference on New Directions in the Humanities. She has also been honoured with the privilege of giving a keynote lecture at the II International Congress of the Faculdades EST. Her published work can be found in *Religião Mídia e Cultura* (2015), *Cinema Journal*, and *The International Journal of Communication and Linguistics Studies*. Formerly, Christine served as a Teaching Assistant at Kingston University and Queen's University as well as serving as an Assistant Editor for *Cinema Journal*. Currently she is working as a Research Assistant at King's University College at The University of Western Ontario.

Laura Braunstein is the Digital Humanities Librarian at Dartmouth College. She is, most recently, the co-editor of *Digital Humanities in the Library: Challenges and Opportunities for Subject Specialists*, and has served on the advisory board for the Schulz Library at the Center for Cartoon Studies in White River Junction, Vermont. She also constructs crossword puzzles, and is the cofounder of The Inkubator, a project to publish puzzles by women – cis women, trans women, and woman-aligned constructors.

Harry Candelario is an artist from North Carollina. Harry has spent time working in the Marvel Comics bullpen as both a penciller and inker for over 13 years.

Scott Cederlund is a recovering English literature major, spending the past 14 years writing about comics. Truthfully, he just doesn't know what to do with his time other than writing about comics. He currently is a contributing editor at Panel Patter (www.panelpatter.com). Scott can be found on Twitter at @scottcederlund.

Carolyn Cocca, Ph.D., is Professor of Politics, Economics, and Law at the State University of New York, College at Old Westbury and author of the Eisner Award-winning *Superwomen: Gender, Power, and Representation*. Her latest book is *Wonder Woman and Captain Marvel: Militarism and Feminism in Comics and Film*. She is also the author of *Jailbait: The Politics of Statutory Rape Laws in the United States* and the editor of *Adolescent Sexuality*. She has written numerous articles and book chapters about gender, sexuality, and the law as well as about gender, sexuality, and superhero comics.

Fraser Coffeen is co-host of the podcast Creepy History (Twitter: @CreepyHist). As a writer, his work has been featured on SBNation affiliate Bloody Elbow where he is a former staff writer, in One Night Only Magazine, and in Horror Homeroom's "Friday the 13th at 40" special issue. Fraser has previously taught and presented on comics for StoryStudio Chicago, as well as the Chicago Public Library where he was a speaker at multiple events, including their annual teen conference "Bam! The Power of Comics and Graphics." His first work with comics came as the model for Mark and Jason in Alex Ross's "Battle of the Planets" art. Fraser has held many jobs including professional wrestling ring announcer, Human Blockhead, theater blood effects artist, and more. He is on Twitter @FCoffeen and Instagram @frasercoffeen.

Sarah Cooke has been a lover of geek culture all her life. She started watching Star Trek at five years old and never looked back. She is a blogger for Marvel and has interviewed many high-profile comic book creators. She has also blogged and reported for DC Comics, CBR, ScreenRant, Den of Geek, Women Write About Comics, and others. She is the co-founder of She-Fi: Ladies Who Love Sci-Fi, an online community for female-identifying and non-binary fans of geek culture.

Enrique del Rey Cabero obtained his Ph.D. in Artistic Creation, Audiovisual and Critical Reflection from the University of Granada. He is currently Lecturer in Hispanic Studies at the University of Exeter and co-convenor of the Oxford Comics Network at the Oxford Research Centre in the Humanities (TORCH), University of Oxford. He has published on comics, literature and applied linguistics in journals such as *The Comics Grid*, *Revista Española de Lingüística Aplicada*, *Journal of Iberian and Latin American Research* and *CuCo. Cuadernos de Cómic*. He is the co-editor of *Dúplex. Cómic y poesía* (2020), co-author *of Studying Comics & Graphic Novels: A guide* (2021) and author of a book on experimental comics and book formats, *(Des)montando el libro. Del comic multilineal al comic objeto* (2021). @enrique_del_rey

Michael James Griffin II is an Upper School Humanities Instructor at The Mount Vernon School in Atlanta, GA where he teaches courses on 19th-21st century literature, writing, and visual communication.

Jeffrey Hayes, Ph.D., earned his doctorate in 2016 from the University of Alabama, and he is an instructor and education specialist. His research and teaching is focused on improving secondary classroom teacher training which includes getting more discussion of comics and pop culture into the curriculum. Twitter: @jldprod2002

Christopher Haynes, Ph.D., is Director of Learning Experience Design in the Office for Academic Innovation at the University of Colorado Boulder. He is also an adjunct instructor for the Division of Continuing Education, where he teaches online courses on fandom, comic books, and popular culture in the digital age. Dr. Haynes received his Ph.D. in English Literature from CU Boulder in 2017, and has published on the future of higher education in *Inside Higher Ed* and *Hybrid Pedagogy*. You can find him on Twitter @_chrishaynes.

Jason Kahler earned his Ph.D. in Composition and Rhetoric from Wayne State University. He developed his love of comics long before that, starting with an issue of "Fantastic Four" that he bought while camping when he was ten years old. His scholarship focuses on writing pedagogy, popular culture, and technology, and he's written reviews and criticism for several comic book websites. Dr. Kahler is currently working on a book about the depiction of disability in comics, which started from several conference papers about his favorite character, Daredevil. He teaches and writes in the American Midwest.

A. David Lewis, Ph.D., has worked in the field of Comics Studies for the past twenty years and has lectured nationally on the subjects of Graphic Medicine, Graphic Religion, and literary theory pertaining to comics. He serves as a college educator in the Greater Boston area and writes the ongoing adventures of *Kismet, Man of Fate*, the world's first Muslim superhero. Dr. Lewis is the co-editor on several volumes of comics research and author of the Eisner Award-nominated *American Comics, Literary Theory, and Religion: The Superhero Afterlife*. In addition to a tenure on the Comics Studies Society Executive Board, he is also the President of the nonprofit Comics for Youth Refugees Incorporated Collective (CYRIC) and a founding member of Sacred and Sequential. Dr. Lewis can be found on Twitter as @adlewis or through his website www.captionbox.net.

Brian LeTendre is a writer and podcaster who created and co-hosted the *Secret Identity* comics podcast from 2006-2017, producing over 800 episodes and 2000 hours of programming. During that run, he and his partner Matt Herring interviewed hundreds of comic creators. From 2008-2010, Brian was a contributor to Comic Book Resources, writing over 100 articles for them, many of which featured interviews with comic creators and game designers. Brian wrote the podcasting how-to book *Making Ear Candy* in 2013, a second edition of which was released in 2017. He currently can be heard co-hosting two music podcasts, *Thrash It Out* and *Power Chords*. He also writes horror, and is the author of the *Parted Veil* series and the co-author of the *Woodsview Murders* series {with Jolene Haley}. You can keep up with Brian on Twitter @seebrianwrite, or on his blog at seebrianwrite.com.

Ryan K Lindsay is an award-winning Australian comic writer. He has written: *Eternal* with Eric Zawadzki through Black Mask Studios; *Headspace* with Zawadzki and Sebastian Piriz through Monkeybrain Comics / IDW; *Beautiful Canvas* through Black Mask Studios; *Deer Editor* through his own 'Four color Ray Gun' imprint along with a handful of Kickstarter successes and *Chum* through ComixTribe, all with Sami Kivela. His other comics include: Aurealis and Ledger Award winning *Negative Space* with Owen Gieni through Dark Horse Comics, and a variety of other one-shots and shorts. He's written / edited analytical texts, including *The Devil is in the Details: Examining Matt Murdock and Daredevil* through Sequart, and had essays published in *Criminal*, *Godzilla*, *Sheltered*, *Strange Nation*, and *Crime Factory*. He's also written comic analysis / reviews for CBR, The Weekly Crisis, and GestaltMash, and sometimes still does this at ryanklindsay.com and on twitter as @ryanklindsay. He is Australian, and when not being a family man, he hones his writing skills by sacrificing blood wombats to the outback spider fight clubs.

Chris McGunnigle received his Ph.D. in 2016 from the University of Louisiana at Lafayette, focusing on New Media Rhetoric. His dissertation analyzed the relationship between magic and modern multimedia in the works of Scottish graphic narrative creator Grant Morrison. In 2018, he was hired as a fulltime instructor at Seton Hall University in New Jersey and assumed the position of Social Media and Communication Coordinator for the *Northeast Popular & American Culture Association in 2020*. Topics from his published works include the cyborg gaze in cyberpunk fiction, fantasy cartography, and genderswapping cosplay. In his downtime, he blogs about various topics in teaching. His blog can be found at doctormcg.wordpress.com/blog/.

Michael Moccio has over five years experience working in the comic book publishing world at companies including NBC Universal, Scholastic, BOOM! Studios, Archie Comics, and Diamond Comic Distributors. He is a freelance comic book editor who has worked with creators such as R.L. Stine and Patrick McHale. He wrote over 200 reviews for Eisner Award-winning website Newsarama, where his average review rating was 6.8. He currently works at NBC Universal as an Editor in the Publishing Department overseeing a variety of licensees and publishing formats, including comics and graphic novels. You can find his hot takes on comics and more on Twitter at @MiMoccio and see his credits at www.michaelmoccio.com.

Hassan Otsmane-Elhaou is the is the editor behind the Eisner-winning *PanelxPanel* magazine, and *Strip Panel Naked* webseries. He's also an editor and letterer of comics, like *Shanghai Red, The Lone Ranger, Red Sonja, Black Mage* and more. He's usually found reading too much into comics, or lost in a field with his dog. His website is hassanoe.co.uk, and he's on Twitter @HassanOE.

Hervé Saint-Louis is an assistant professor of emerging media at the Université du Québec à Chicoutimi (UQAC) in Saguenay, Canada. He researches usable security (a branch of human-computer interaction) and specializes in the philosophy of authentication, privacy, confidentiality, and information policy. A recent doctoral graduate from the University of Toronto's Faculty of Information, Saint-Louis is a cartoonist and the creator of Johnny Bullet, a classic-styled adventure comic strip about a 1970s auto-racer and his ride. Johnny Bullet is currently published as a web comic at ComicBookBin.com, the news and review site Saint-Louis founded in 2002. ComicBookBin's writers have reviewed several thousand comics from North America, Asia, Europe, and more. Before academia, Saint-Louis trained as an animator and did cartoon animation for corporate clients at Toon Doctor, his studio.

Andy Schmidt, former Senior Editor at IDW Publishing, former Editor at Marvel Comics, and former Director of Intellectual Property and Brand Design at Hasbro, is also the founder of Comics Experience, the world's largest online comic book education platform. During his nearly six years at Marvel Comics, Andy edited such popular comic books as *X-Men, X-Factor, Alias, Secret War, Captain America: The Chosen, Iron Man / Captain America: Casualties of War, Avengers Classic*, and the *Annihilation* saga. As an assistant and associate editor, Andy worked on nearly every major character in the Marvel canon, from Spider-Man to the Avengers and Fantastic Four. In 2008, Andy wrote an authoritative, Eagle Award-winning book about making comics: *The Insider's Guide to Creating Comics and Graphic Novels*, published by Impact Books, and followed up with *The Comics Experience Guide to Writing Comics: Scripting Your Story Ideas from Start to Finish* in 2018. Andy lives in Kentucky with his wife, two sons, and super dope dog.

Stephen Sharar is an artist and comic store owner from Saginaw, Michigan.

Suman Sigroha, Ph.D., is a researcher and teacher at one of the premier Technical Institutes in India. With her training in the field of literary studies and also in psychology, she engages with texts through psycho-social concepts like stereotyping, implicit bias, memory and representation. She deals with intersections of art, history, and fiction, besides myths, oral history, and popular fiction. She finds the journey from text to motion picture fascinating and tries to unravel its various facets with her students at IIT Mandi, India. Her recent research focuses on contemporary literature from troubled regions of India, rich with unsettling questions about nationalism, belonging, identity, and ideals of love amidst terrorism and militarization. She has published in various national and international journals and presented at various forums. She has recently contributed to and co-edited *Translational Research and Applied Psychology in India* (SAGE, 2019).

Philip Smith is Associate Chair of Liberal Arts and Professor of English at Savannah College of Art and Design. He is author of *Reading Art Spiegelman*, *Shakespeare in Singapore*, and *Printing Terror: American Horror Comics as Cold War Commentary and Critique*. He is coeditor of *Firefly Revisited: Essays on Joss Whedon's Classic Series, Gender and the Superhero Narrative*, and *The Search for Understanding: Elie Wiesel's Literary Works*. He is editor in chief of *Literature Compass*.

Ben Towle is a four-time Eisner-nominated cartoonist currently working on his next graphic novel, *Four Fisted Tales*, a collection of true-life stories of animals in combat forthcoming from Dead Reckoning, the graphic novel imprint of The Naval Institute Press. His previous work, the rollicking nautical fantasy comic, *Oyster War,* was published by Oni Press in 2015. His other work includes *Amelia Earhart: This Broad Ocean* (with Sarah Stewart Taylor), a graphic novel for young adults (Disney/Hyperion Books 2010) which received accolades from such publications as *The New York Times* and *Publishers Weekly* and was a Junior Library Guild selection, as well as the historical fiction graphic novel *Midnight Sun* and a volume of comics folk tales, *Farewell, Georgia*. His website is benzilla.com and he's on Twitter @ben_towle.

ALSO FROM **SEQUART**

THE BRITISH INVASION: ALAN MOORE, NEIL GAIMAN, GRANT MORRISON, AND THE
    INVENTION OF THE MODERN COMIC BOOK WRITER
HUMANS AND PARAGONS: ESSAYS ON SUPER-HERO JUSTICE
MOVING PANELS: TRANSLATING COMICS TO FILM

 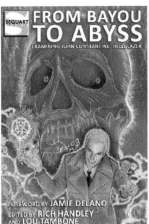 

MUSINGS ON MONSTERS: OBSERVATIONS ON THE WORLD OF CLASSIC HORROR
FROM BAYOU TO ABYSS: EXAMINING JOHN CONSTANTINE, HELLBLAZER
CLASSICS ON INFINITE EARTHS: THE JUSTICE LEAGUE AND DC CROSSOVER CANON

BOOKS ON SCI-FI FRANCHISES:

Somewhere Beyond the Heavens: Exploring Battlestar Galactica

The Cyberpunk Nexus: Exploring the Blade Runner Universe

The Sacred Scrolls: Comics on the Planet of the Apes

Bright Lights, Ape City: Examining the Planet of the Apes Mythos

New Life and New Civilizations: Exploring Star Trek Comics

A Long Time Ago: Exploring the Star Wars Cinematic Universe

A Galaxy Far, Far Away: Exploring Star Wars Comics

A More Civilized Age: Exploring the Star Wars Expanded Universe

The Weirdest Sci-Fi Comic Ever Made: Understanding Jack Kirby's *2001: A Space Odyssey*

BOOKS ON GRANT MORRISON:

Grant Morrison: The Early Years

Our Sentence is Up: Seeing Grant Morrison's *The Invisibles*

Curing the Postmodern Blues: Reading Grant Morrison and Chris Weston's *The Filth* in the 21st Century

The Anatomy of Zur-en-Arrh: Understanding Grant Morrison's Batman

BOOKS ON WARREN ELLIS:

Shot in the Face: A Savage Journey to the Heart of *Transmetropolitan*

Keeping the World Strange: A *Planetary* Guide

Voyage in Noise: Warren Ellis and the Demise of Western Civilization

Warren Ellis: The Captured Ghosts Interviews

ON TV AND MOVIES:

Mutant Cinema: The X-Men Trilogy from Comics to Screen

Gotham City 14 Miles: 14 Essays on Why the 1960s Batman TV Series Matters

Improving the Foundations: *Batman Begins* from Comics to Screen

Time is a Flat Circle: Examining *True Detective*, Season One

OTHER BOOKS:

Judging Dredd: Examining the World of Judge Dredd

The Mignolaverse: Hellboy and the Comics Art of Mike Mignola

Moving Target: The History and Evolution of Green Arrow

The Devil is in the Details: Examining Matt Murdock and Daredevil

Teenagers from the Future: Essays on the Legion of Super-Heroes

The Best There is at What He Does: Examining Chris Claremont's X-Men

And the Universe so Big: Understanding *Batman: The Killing Joke*

Minutes to Midnight: Twelve Essays on *Watchmen*

When Manga Came to America: Super-Hero Revisionism in *Mai, the Psychic Girl*

The Future of Comics, The Future of Men: Matt Fraction's *Casanova*

DOCUMENTARY FILMS:

Diagram for Delinquents

She Makes Comics

The Image Revolution

Neil Gaiman: Dream Dangerously

Grant Morrison: Talking with Gods

Warren Ellis: Captured Ghosts

Comics in Focus: Chris Claremont's X-Men

For more information and for exclusive content, visit Sequart.org.

Printed in Great Britain
by Amazon